Why I left
the Contemporary Christian Music
movement

Why I left the Contemporary Christian Music movement

Confessions of a former worship leader

Dan Lucarini

EP BOOKS
Faverdale North, Darlington, DL3 0PH, England

e-mail: sales@epbooks.org
web:http://www.epbooks.org

EP BOOKS USA
P. O. Box 614, Carlisle, PA 17013, USA

e-mail: usasales@epbooks.org
web: http://www.epbooks.us

First published 2002
Nineteenth impression 2007
Twentieth impression 2010

British Library Cataloguing in Publication Data available

ISBN-13 978-0-85234-517-7   ISBN 0-85234-517-8

Printed and bound in the United States of America.

Dedication

This book is dedicated to the authors, pastors, music ministers and other church leaders who came before me. They never ceased to warn us about the dangers of rock music to a Christian; but we did not take heed. They had the courage to confront others in the church who defended every controversial and sensual music style; but in return we heaped scorn upon them. When they dared to oppose the contemporary music invasion into the church service itself, we called them legalists and worse. Many have sacrificed popularity and seen their ministry opportunities limited, because their consciences dictated they must take a stand. To them, we owe an apology and a debt of gratitude. This book is an attempt to pay a small portion of that debt.

Acknowledgements

To my wife Judy — for never giving up on me through all the struggles related in the pages of this book, and for being my 'early warning system' against everything that exalts itself against the knowledge of God. Your fervent prayers and tears before the Lord have finally been honoured. I love you! To Chris, Amanda and Danette — for your patience and understanding with your Dad, and for helping me to make this book more relevant to your generation. To Scott and Suzette Burtoft — for sharing your own struggle, and for your inspiration and prayers.

To Troy Self, my music pastor and friend — for your enthusiastic support of this project from the very beginning, and for your personal ministry to my family. To Craig Scott, my pastor and friend — for taking a strong stand on music issues, and for providing me with a wealth of great material for this book from your preaching.

To Pastor Roger Fay — for being so kind as to ask me about the manuscript one day at Willis Metcalfe's house in Ripon, North Yorkshire, and for introducing it to Evangelical Press. To Art Hockman and the Home Builders' Sunday school class at Woodside — for allowing me to test the manuscript on you, and for continual prayer.

To Diane Landry — for generously donating your time to edit the rough draft into a readable document, and for your many contributions to the final text. To David Leitch — for your generosity in reviewing the manuscript *pro bono*. To David, Anthony and Pete — thanks for putting up with this novice author.

And to my Lord and Saviour Jesus Christ: 'I will praise you, O Lord, among the peoples; I will sing to you among the nations. For your mercy reaches unto the heavens, and your truth unto the clouds. Be exalted, O God, above the heavens; let your glory be above all the earth!' (Psalm 57:9-11).

Contents

Foreword

Music has often been a 'hot potato' in the life of the Christian church, and the subject may never have been more controversial than during the past fifty years.

At one end of the spectrum, there are those who tell us that the only words that should be sung in the church are those forming the Old Testament psalms — and that they should be sung without any musical accompaniment. At the other end, there are those who say that any kind of music — rock, pop, jazz, punk, country and western, rap, or whatever 'turns people on' is perfectly legitimate for use in worship and evangelism.

Dan Lucarini never approached the first of these extremes, but he came within touching distance of the second, and it is from his deeply involved experience of the modern music scene, secular and otherwise, that this book is written.

The author's honest sharing of his own spiritual and musical journey prepares the way for his assessment of what he sees to be a major problem in today's church — and makes it more difficult to deny that he is on to something.

This book will undoubtedly raise many hackles, but Lucarini's direct and uncompromising style is harnessed to a gracious spirit concerned with nothing else but God's glory. This is nowhere more evident than in his warm and wise treatment of the subject of worship and ministry.

John Calvin once wrote, 'We know by experience that music has a secret and almost incredible power to move hearts.' The Reformer was right — and we should therefore give its use in the life of the church serious and God-centred attention. I pray that this book will help us to do so.

John Blanchard

1.
Saving butterflies from the storm

God gave my wife Judy two wonderful gifts that I do not have: a very sensitive spiritual antenna and the ability to quickly understand situations for what they really are. In our twenty-one years of marriage, I have been constantly amazed (and grateful) at how she is able to discern the long-term negative effects of seemingly positive new trends and fashions in the church. On the other hand, her God-given insight has also made her particularly sensitive to the hurting and wounded souls in the church.

In 1993, Judy and I were on vacation in Muskegon, Michigan, USA, when a violent summer storm blew in over Lake Michigan with fierce winds, driving rain and pounding surf. After the storm, we were walking on the beach when Judy suddenly noticed monarch butterflies half-buried in the sand at her feet. We looked around and saw literally hundreds of butterflies scattered on the beach.

At first they all appeared to be dead. Judy bent over and nudged one, and to our surprise it tried to move, and escape by flying. But its wings were soaked and weighed down with sand particles, and it could not break free in its own strength. The gale force winds had blown it onto the beach and left its wings torn and tattered.

We were both overcome with compassion for this poor butterfly. It would never survive unless someone rescued it. Judy gently picked it up, and with great care brushed sand from its wings and held it in the sunlight to dry. After a few moments, the wings began to move, slowly at first, then a bit faster. She showed this to me and we had a glimmer of hope that it might survive. But the butterfly still needed to fly on its own in order to live.

A gentle breeze was blowing off the lake, the kind that often follows a violent storm. She tossed the butterfly up into the breeze, and we watched as it began to flutter and try to fly. It dipped and weaved, and I thought it would crash. But suddenly, its wings regained strength and it was able to fly to a nearby plant. The butterfly rescue worked! We went up and down the beach, frantically trying to rescue as many more as we could, Judy lifting them out of the sand and brushing them off, me helping them fly again. But they were dying too fast, and sadly we were able to save only a few dozen.

The Christian Contemporary Music movement

Later a local resident tried to explain this strange phenomenon to me. He believed the storm had blown the butterflies across the lake all the way from Wisconsin, and dumped them on our beach. The butterflies were overwhelmed by the strong winds ahead of the storm and were swept along, powerless to resist. They never saw it coming.

Judy once likened the Contemporary Christian Music (CCM) movement to that mighty storm. In the 1990s, this movement blew into our church services accompanied by powerful forces, and anyone who got in the way was like the butterfly, swept away by its proponents, wounded during the violent journey, and finally dumped on the beach to perish. Some may never fly again, because their spirits were too tattered and torn by the storm's forces. Others had their souls weighed down by the immorality, deception and divisiveness that accompanied the CCM storm.

I am a former contemporary praise and worship leader. I was neither famous nor well known, simply a foot soldier who spent several years inside the movement acting as a CCM change agent, leading churches through the difficult transition from traditional services into contemporary praise and worship. Throughout those years, I enthusiastically promoted the acceptance of CCM into the weekly services at evangelical and fundamental churches. I thought it was the right thing to do for God and for the church.

Two years ago I left the movement after God opened my eyes to the deceptions and dangers within it (which I will describe in detail later in this book). I am telling my story because I want to rescue the butterflies that have been wounded by the CCM storm. I also want to warn churches with traditional music services where they are heading if they are considering a switch to a contemporary worship service. To those who want to stand against such a change, I hope to provide encouragement and answers based on biblical principles. This book will help them to answer the proponents of CCM and to refute their arguments.

I know there are others within that movement who, like me, are attracted to the music but are troubled by the problems they see and do not know how to express their concerns. Where can they go for help and encouragement? Plenty of material has already been written about the problem of using CCM in the church. But most of that material was written by individuals who were never proponents of CCM or part of the movement. The Contemporaries I know would not read such material because of their prejudice towards anyone who is labelled as a 'fundamentalist' or 'traditionalist', whom perhaps they have characterized unfairly as holding on to old, dead musical traditions.

Personal involvement

I, on the other hand, can offer a genuine 'in the trenches' view of the attitudes and motives inside the movement, because I was deeply involved until recently. Some Contemporaries are quick to use the generation gap as an excuse to dismiss criticism of their music by elders, claiming they do not like CCM because they are from a different generation. But that will not work with me. I experienced my share of loud and vulgar rock music in the 1970s; I understand 'in your face' music styles. The worst music of today is but an extension of what we started back then. When you read this book I hope you will agree that no one can dismiss me as being a 'dyed in the wool' traditionalist who is stuck in the old ways.

Let me set your expectations for this book. It is not meant to be an exhaustive theological discussion of music in the Bible and the church. But I will appeal constantly to God's Word as the final authority for our worship practices and lifestyles; readers who do not share this view of Scripture, therefore, may find my arguments less than convincing. Likewise, we will not cover the issue of the rock music beat and its controversial effects on human physiology. Others have written and preached well enough on those subjects. This book does not specifically address the issue of what music styles you ought to listen to in your own private time, although I believe every Christian can find benefits from the warnings and principles concerning public worship.

Rather, we will focus on the charge that mixing certain contemporary music styles into our worship services is at best a questionable practice for the saints of God, and at worst can lead to division, self-indulgence and immorality. Any criticism found in these pages is generally directed at those responsible for leading the CCM charge, not at the average worshipper.

Here is a key to understanding some special terms we will use.

- *CCM*: Contemporary Christian Music. Specifically, this includes music styles such as soft rock, pop/rock, easy listening or classic rock, but could also include other forms of heavily syncopated music with rock influences such as jazz, rap, blues, hip-hop, punk, ska or modern country & western.
- *P&W*: the Praise and Worship movement of CCM. This music style also has a strong rock influence. Some of the best-known sources for this music are Integrity Hosanna, Vineyard and Maranatha Music.
- *Contemporaries*: Christians who prefer CCM for praise and worship in church services. This is not meant as a derogatory label in any way, but only as a method of distinguishing musically one Christian from the other.
- *The Traditionals*: Christians who prefer traditional or conservative music in church services; by 'conservative' is meant that the music is generally considered to be non-controversial and safe. Our definition includes hymns, traditional songs and those contemporary music styles that do not use rock or other musical influences that emphasize sensuality. The term 'traditional' has become a derogatory label in some CCM circles but here we hope to reclaim the positive meaning of the word.

It is my prayer that all that is written here will glorify God the Father and our Lord Jesus Christ, and that it will stimulate respectful dialogue within the body of Christ. My remarks are not intended to offend any Christian who is promoting or is otherwise involved in a contemporary music ministry. My friends will tell you that I do *not* like confrontation, but try both to be a peacemaker and to live in peace. Having said that, I realize my story and my conclusions will be a thorn in the side of some Christians. If you want to stir up controversy in the church, just bring up the subject of musical styles.

I also understand that some Christian friends who worked with me in past music ministries will be surprised, and even shocked, at my change of mind about CCM. They saw me perform it in church and work hard behind the scenes for its acceptance. We had good experiences together and were sincere about our ministry. It is my prayer that they will consider all that is said here and then examine their own role in promoting CCM.

Powerful stronghold

I realize I am also challenging a *very powerful stronghold* in the church. CCM is well entrenched now, perhaps even the favoured music style in the majority of fundamental and evangelical church services. CCM has taken deep root in the lives of many believers, and some will find what they read here very painful because it will tug hard on that root. Some pastors will not like what I have to say because they too have embraced this movement. But I believe that the use of CCM in praise and worship is a man-made phenomenon and should be exposed as such because it lacks a strong biblical foundation and ignores God's instructions for acceptable worship. Using it for worship has produced wrong attitudes and encouraged carnal lifestyles; both are damaging the unity and effectiveness of Christians. I also believe the real motive for adopting CCM for praise and worship was not, as we were often told, to evangelize those from outside the church, but was rooted in a need to satisfy our own desires for *our* favourite music. Finally, we have come to the point where even our definition of worship has very little resemblance to its biblical meaning. So I can no longer be silent.

At this point, the reader may already have concluded that I am one of those people who believes *everything* about CCM is bad. That is not the case! This book documents my personal experience with the spiritual dangers and non-biblical philosophies found within contemporary P&W. I know there are many sincere Christians involved in the movement, convinced they are doing God's will and truly concerned that he receives the glory. I also believe there is good music to be found within CCM, music with biblically sound lyrics and beautiful melodies, which, if separated from the incessant rock beat and the worldly performance styles, would be acceptable for use in worship.

If you are involved in the contemporary P&W movement within your church, I do not condemn you! I am very sensitive to Jesus' command in Matthew 7:1-5 and Luke 6:42 that we should not judge! He went on to say that we must first remove the beam from our own eye, and only *then* will we see clearly! I have tried to remove the telephone poles from my own eyes before I presumed to call anyone else to account.

Although I will share freely my convictions and advice, nothing said in this book should be construed as being a rule by which I expect other Christians to live. Making new rules would be tantamount to legalism, and I (following the example of the apostle Paul) have no desire to weigh anyone down with regulations that 'indeed have an appearance of wisdom in self-imposed religion, false humility, and neglect of the body, but are of no value against the indulgence of the flesh' (Colossians 2:23).

This is a family fight, a disagreement between brothers and sisters in Christ, whom I care enough about to warn against any involvement in such an unproductive and divisive movement. I want to challenge Contemporaries to consider their role in CCM P&W and show them a *better* way. I would ask, therefore, that this testimony is given a fair and complete reading *before* any judgement is made.

2.
My story

Christ saved me when I was twenty-three years of age. Up until that turning point in my life, I was very active in the rock and pop music world and its associated immoral lifestyle. It was not always like that. My parents were dedicated members of the United Methodist Church; I was baptized as an infant, confirmed at age twelve, and went to Sunday school, but I was not saved according to the Bible's definition. I rebelled against the teachings of the church and whenever I was given the chance to perform special music there, I would pick a contemporary pseudo-religious song such as George Harrison's 'My Sweet Lord' or the politically correct 'Abraham Martin and John'. From age thirteen onwards, I performed with bands, playing the keyboards and singing lead or background vocals; I wrote songs; and I listened to rock music several hours a day. My main musical influences were Billy Joel, Deep Purple, Chicago and Elton John. I went to college on a music scholarship and spent a year in a theory and composition programme before changing my main subject to journalism. In college I promoted rock concerts for acts such as Fleetwood Mac, America, Emerson Lake & Palmer, and Stephen Stills.

Before Christ saved me, several people witnessed to me and challenged me to read the Word of God. That convinced me that I was living a sinful life. The Bible was enough; no one needed rock music to attract me to the gospel! Even as an unbeliever I had a sense that God was not to be associated with my music. My wife-to-be Judy took me to see a film called *A Distant Thunder*, which was about the great tribulation. Afterwards, I realized that I was lost and heading for an eternity in hell. I was very sorry for disobeying God, repented of my ways and asked God for forgiveness. I placed my faith in the risen Lord and Saviour Jesus Christ who gave me the power to become a child of God (John 1:12). I was 'born again' and immediately my life began to change.

Convicted by the Holy Spirit

The Holy Spirit convicted me to deal with the immorality in my life. Through a combination of the power of Christ, prayer, Bible study and accountability to Christians around me, I was able to turn away from the rock music, drugs, cigarettes, alcohol and sexual immorality that had marked my life before Jesus. I joined Judy's church, one that took a strong stand against rock music. God knew this was exactly what I needed to fight against the desires of my sinful nature, which were easily stirred up by rock music.

Shortly after my conversion, I had my first musical experience as a born-again believer. Our church joined several others to host an area-wide evangelistic crusade at the county fairgrounds. Each of the churches was asked to send choir members to participate in a big crusade choir that would sing each night. Judy and my future mother-in-law (the choir director at our church) both encouraged me to get involved, thinking it would be a great way for me to use some of my talents while learning about good Christian music. I agreed enthusiastically and Judy accompanied me to the first practice session where I took my place in the bass section and sang loud and in tune. There were hundreds of people in the choir and they sounded great to me! The choir leader mentioned there would be bass and baritone solos, and I was ready to audition. I was genuinely thrilled to be involved in a music programme that was part of God's work.

Get your hair cut!

When practice ended, the choir leader asked both myself and the man standing beside me to come forward and speak with him. My companion could sing too, so I presumed that the leader had singled us out to audition for the solos. What happened next could have driven me away from the Lord. The leader told us that our hair was too long for the choir and we should not come back unless we had it cut to a certain length. I was devastated. I think I may have asked him exactly how short my hair should be because I had no idea. This was all very new to me. I walked off the platform, feeling rejected by God. Judy asked me what was wrong and I told her. I recall making a sarcastic remark that the leader was just jealous of my full head of hair because *he* was almost bald.

However, I soon discovered one of the great benefits of being really, truly born again — the Holy Spirit. Praise the Lord! His presence helped me to become better, instead of bitter. I submitted (a new thing for me), got my hair cut to specification and was back in the choir the next night. The leader and I did not discuss the matter further at that time, but there is an amazing ending to this story. Recently, while attending a sacred music conference in South Carolina with my music pastor, I related this story to him. When I told him the name of the choir leader, he told me that same person was there at the conference and then pointed him out to me! We met and I told him the story.

He immediately apologized if there had been any offence and I think he was very relieved to hear how God used that incident for good. As we talked, I learned about his music ministry and the great sacrifices he and his wife had made to be part of an evangelistic team. They are truly great musical servants of God yet in my ignorance I had cast him as a symbol of legalism. Another lesson learned!

For a time after my conversion, I found it difficult to give up 'my' rock music, which, with its accompanying lifestyle, had for so many years defined my identity and was the source of much of my self-esteem. Rock music also had a strong grasp on my flesh, and tearing it away was painful. Some Christians say that rock music has no effect on them physically but I can assure you that it affected me. I believe its physical hold came about because rock music was associated with every flagrant sin of the flesh I had committed and even a hint of that music was enough to stir up memories of those ungodly associations. But Jesus Christ promised to provide all my needs, and so I asked him to replace my old music with new music that was pleasing to him. It took over a year but, praise God, I began to see answers to my prayer.

A new song

It was a miracle to me! I grew to love the great hymns of the faith and the simple, heartfelt choruses we sang at church. The sincerity and the purity of this music overwhelmed me. (In contrast, my favourite classic rock music now seemed so profane, so loud and obnoxious.) I joined the choir. The Lord even gave me the ability to write new songs dedicated to him. Before he came into my life, I had written about fifty songs. Song writing was a passion of mine and now I wanted to use this passion for Christ. I can truly testify to you that he put a new song in my heart.

Yet I still had to deal with the lingering influence of my musical background on the new songs I wrote. I turned everything into a pop/rock-style song. I rearranged Ralph Carmichael's classic 'He's Everything to Me' into a bluesy 6/8 tempo, complete with blues riffs (short repeated musical phrases) on the piano and vocal styling right out of the public bars where I used to perform. I found it odd that no one at the church confronted me about it. I was thankful for their gracious spirit but now I wonder what would have happened if someone had taken me aside then and explained the danger of this approach.

As I grew in the Lord and demonstrated faithfulness to him, eventually I was given the privilege of leading the services. I inherited this ministry from my father-in-law, a man of great faith who practises real obedience to God's will and who I consider to be an important role model for my life. This was my first opportunity to lead God's people in praise and worship. I purposed to be careful behind the pulpit and show respect for the traditional music. Our music styles and choices were conservative, using the hymnals, organ, piano and choir. The services followed the usual American Protestant format: prelude, opening hymn, prayer, announcements, choir, offertory, hymn, special music, sermon, invitation hymn and closing word. We occasionally sang a contemporary chorus in the Sunday evening service but were very careful not to use any with a rock music style. We worked hard to keep the emphasis on praise to God, not on the performer or the performance. Some soloists (including me) used background accompaniment tapes, a source of controversy because some tapes had noticeable rock beats or used unsaved musicians.

Then I moved my family to a nearby town and we joined a church there. The services were similar to the previous church, very conservative. But there seemed to be a deadness in the worship service; everything seemed to be done by rote, not out of love or passion for God. Judy and I longed for a worship time that was real, alive and relevant; one that demonstrated an intimate relationship with Christ. We encountered several other members who felt the same way and wanted to revive the service by using some new music and trying some different orders of service. We all had something in common: each of us had been exposed to contemporary worship music through a variety of venues such as the Concerts of Prayer[1] or CCM concerts.

Desire to worship

I believe this desire for genuine worship is one of the primary reasons why people such as us leave conservative churches for contemporary ones. Each of us longs for a deeper, stronger relationship with our Lord and Saviour manifested through 'genuine' worship (as contrasted to the 'fake' worship we felt characterized the traditional church service) and we are led to believe this can be gained or enhanced through music. I understand now that this is not the case, and that to develop an intimate relationship with the Lord we must abide in him daily. If we need the weekly worship service to do that for us, what does that say about our true commitment to discipleship? Are we really just play-acting?

The church had just taken on a new, younger pastor — like myself, from the baby boomer generation (born between 1946 and 1960). At his previous church, the pastor had agreed to have a worship band during the Sunday service. However, far from producing favourable results, it had in fact produced division. Nevertheless, he approved of the changes we wanted to make, thinking he could avoid such division again by proceeding cautiously.

With good intentions and great enthusiasm, we held special churchwide meetings to discuss our proposed changes to the music ministry. This was when I first encountered the resistance of Traditionals, coming from many of the older members and families who had been in the church for the longest time. For every objection raised, our group of budding Contemporaries had an assuring answer. No, we weren't going to bring a drum set into the church. Yes, we would still sing mostly hymns. We would use the current pianist and organist. Everything would be done decently and in order. The Traditionals were not swayed by our arguments, but they were unable to articulate their concerns well enough to dissuade us. Frankly, I felt they were just holding on to traditions and had no biblical foundation for their objections. (I conveniently overlooked the fact that neither did we!) On the other hand, we had all the clever arguments and we were not going to be denied. There was a sense of 'manifest destiny' on our side, that musical change was inevitable and even critical to the survival of the church.

By the way, have you noticed who usually leads the campaign for CCM acceptance? The Contemporary musicians do! We musicians have the most to gain from a change and we have a vested interest in the outcome. Why? In churches that use traditional styles, the vast majority of contemporary musicians are not involved in music leadership. I wonder how many have felt left out, or longed for the chance to serve God with their musical talents. But the situation is reversed when CCM is brought into the church. With very few exceptions, the Traditional music leadership does not survive the transition and Contemporary musicians take over the music ministry. The Traditional musicians are then the ones feeling useless.

At the same time, Judy (unlike me) was experiencing serious doubts about using CCM in the church service. In her Bible study, she had seen how the Israelites mixed pagan worship practices with God's commanded methods of worshipping him; as a result God severely judged Israel. At the time, she thought it was acceptable to use CCM for private enjoyment and edification; but she also believed that the music style had such strong associations with the world's idols of sex and image that it should not be used during a worship service. I should have listened to her then but I was already caught up in the movement.

Influence of the world

Judy also noticed that some of the people who were going to lead contemporary music and drama had received their creative influences from worldly sources and were actually quite open about it. Wouldn't this have the potential to pollute the people of God? But these same people were also loving and accepting. How then could she question their motives? Her unrocolvcd doubls left her confused and feeling powerless; she tried to warn me but I was not listening.

The church decided to proceed and I was asked to lead the transition from a traditional to a 'blended' service, which I will explain later. But three months into this, a new job took us away to Denver, Colorado, and I was not able to finish what we had started. The church moved ahead with the changes after we left and lost some faithful members in the process.

In Denver, we looked for a church that was fundamental in faith and doctrine but could also meet my desire for some contemporary music in the services and would accept our personal use of CCM. By now, our three children were aged thirteen, ten and eight. We first visited a large non-denominational church recommended by trusted friends back in Ohio. It was our first exposure to a 'seeker-sensitive' driven ministry with a very polished, professional praise and worship team. (A seeker-sensitive ministry is an evangelistic ministry that focuses primarily on the needs of the person seeking God.) Everything about the music was first class, especially the audio equipment, the lighting and the pace of the service. It appealed to me, but Judy and the children felt uncomfortable with the high-tech performance style. We took my father when he visited from Pennsylvania and he was visibly disturbed by this new wave of worship; but I ignored this early warning too. However, I realized the entire family had to be happy with a church so we moved on.

Next, we attended a non-denominational church which had about 100 members. The pastor, again the same age as me, was a former Baptist who had created a seeker-driven church to reach out to the community without the restrictions of the Baptist label. He wanted to reach people who were wounded by experiences with hypocrisy in fundamental churches and who, as a result, had stopped attending church: the so-called 'unchurched'. His philosophy of unconditional love for all people and his drive to have a real passion for God, not to just be religious, appealed to us.

The worship service was already contemporary because the pastor did not want anything that looked like a traditional Baptist service. I joined the music ministry, playing keyboards in the praise band and eventually taking over as worship leader. The pastor had a vision to become the 'church that rocks' and we certainly had some services like that. One Sunday morning, we performed the rowdy Grand Funk Railroad hit 'Some Kind of Wonderful' but used Mark Farner's 'saved' edition in which he changed the words so that the object of his affection was now Jesus. (Changing the lyrics but keeping the music is a standard practice in CCM.) I was easily attracted to this style of music because of my background and my old rock music desires. However, Judy was appalled and walked out in the middle of our irreverent performance.

Once again, praise God for Judy's spiritual antenna. She discerned spirits of rebellion and immorality at work in the church body. In his effort to create a non-judgemental atmosphere, the pastor promoted a 'God accepts us as we are' philosophy, with which CCM seems to go hand in hand. This was a pastor who once accepted tickets to a Doobie Brothers rock concert and defended his choice by claiming that if Jesus were alive today, he would be at this concert because he spent time with sinners. This teaching produced a church that attracted people who wanted God in their lives but did not want to change their lifestyles. Judy saw the hypocrisy and danger in this for our children and for our own marriage. She finally got through to me and we left that church, as well.

The right church?

Next, we thought the Lord had finally led us to the right church. It seemed to be so balanced in all aspects of the ministry (including music) and church life, so solid in doctrine and practice. The pastor was once again around my age but he was more conservative than the previous three pastors. The preaching of the Word was excellent. The music was a blend of the great hymns and Maranatha Music-style choruses. There was a band but the drums and guitars were muted and balanced, not overpowering. Instead of one song leader, there was a singing team of men and women who seemed to have the proper spirit of reverence. 'Wow,' I thought, 'this is the way I always wanted it: good balance in the music ministry.'

The worship team leader needed someone to play the church's synthesizer. So I joined the music ministry and when the leader moved away from the area, I was asked to succeed him. I became responsible for creating and arranging the Sunday morning worship service for a congregation of almost 500. I wrote special musical arrangements, conducted weekly practices, arranged vocals, sang, and played the keyboards. The worship team consisted of between five and seven singers and up to ten instrumentalists on any given Sunday.

Our typical worship service was twenty-five minutes of praise and worship-style songs with prayer interspersed throughout. I also tried to include at least one hymn per week. The worship 'set' (a term borrowed from the secular performance world) was arranged to be a continuous flow of music with no interruptions. That was an important ingredient to maintain the mood. We used a large projection screen for the lyrics and were blessed with a state-of-the-art multimedia system and excellent technicians. We became very good at contemporary praise and worship, and were once complimented by a visiting denominational leader as 'the best in Colorado'.

Another strong musical influence in my life at this time was Promise Keepers, the well-known men's movement based in Colorado. Promise Keeper music uses predominantly rock styles, including classic Seventies-style rock. I attended huge stadium rallies where the Maranatha Men's Band ministered in music.

At this point, I need to confess another motive that drove me to lead contemporary praise and worship. Suddenly, here were all these churches trying to play rock music in their services but performing it so badly! Didn't they realize the unchurched would laugh at their weak attempts and stop coming? I thought that if they were going to use rock, they should ensure it was of the highest quality. I knew exactly how to fix that. Because of my rock and roll background and experiences, I was an expert on how the music should be played. And because of my additional experience as a hymn song-leader, I even thought God was 'calling' me to be the bridge between traditional and contemporary church music.

Under my direction, the worship services progressed from a blend of hymns and 'easy-listening' choruses to a completely contemporary service. I drew my music choices almost exclusively from Integrity Hosanna Music and Maranatha Music. I especially liked the Integrity P&W music because it combined

good pop/rock techniques with sensitivity to the needs of
congregational singing and lyrics that praised God and Jesus
Christ. Our favourite songs for worship were:

Lord I Lift Your Name on High
Shout to the Lord
Mighty is Our God
Lift Up Your Voices
Great is the Lord
Change My Heart O God
Refiner's Fire
Purify My Heart
Give Thanks

There were musicians on the team who wanted to extend
the boundaries of acceptability and try edgier material. 'Edgier'
is a common term used by Contemporaries to describe music
that takes the listeners to the 'edge' of their comfort zone, stretch-
ing them beyond their pre-conceived notions of appropriateness. Some of the singers wanted to use new Vineyard praise
and worship music that contained a great deal of repetition and
beat. The lyrics reflected a charismatic theology that should
have no place in a Baptist church. Our normally humble drummer had an electric drum set that enabled us to control the
sound, but even he constantly wanted to add a strong beat to
every song we played. The electric guitar player, a lover of classic
rock, looked for every chance to play solos or add guitar riffs
where they weren't needed. During our weekly practices, the
praise band would often switch into a rock and roll 'jam session'. As the leader, I could have discouraged this but I chose
instead to indulge my own appetite for rock and roll. To put it
bluntly, I was having fun! As I look back on this, I see how hard
it was to restrain the rock music beast and prevent it from taking
over completely.

A summary

I would like to stop here, take a deep breath and summarize the reasons and motives that led me into the CCM P&W scene. Firstly, CCM used the music style that I was not only very good at, but which also attracted me. Due to my lack of formal training I never felt I fitted in with the 'sacred' musicians. CCM offered me the only opportunity to be the best-trained musician in church and to use that talent for God. Secondly, I have to admit that being a CCM leader was tremendously gratifying to my ego. The respect and adoration given to me was faintly reminiscent of the rock star power I experienced as an unsaved performer. But I was blinded to this because the gratification was packaged in an 'acceptable Christian' format.

Thirdly, I was with pastors who wanted this music in church and who influenced me greatly. I was raised in a military family, which left me with a temperament predisposed to pleasing those in authority. There is a serious leadership issue involved in the acceptance and promotion of CCM in church. Yes, I am responsible for my choices and I'm not trying to place blame anywhere else. But there are many men like me in churches, willing to follow the pastor wherever he leads us (after all, pastor means shepherd). If the pastor wants to change the music, who will stand up to him? Certainly not me.

The 'seeker-sensitive' church

Meanwhile, our pastor took up a ministry position in the east of America. The denominational leadership helped us select a new pastor, whose previous experience was starting a community church in Arizona patterned after the model espoused by Rick Warren in his book *The Purpose Driven Church*. The previous pastor had given me a copy to read so I was already familiar with Pastor Warren's philosophy of ministry. He favoured a seeker-sensitive ministry, where the church and its services are designed specifically to meet the 'felt needs' of the person who is seeking God.

What are those needs and what music is best suited to meet them? Pastor Warren defines this in his book:

> We use the style of music the majority of people in our church listen to on the radio. They like bright, happy, cheerful music with a strong beat. Their ears are accustomed to music with a strong bass line and rhythm.
>
> For the first time in history, there exists a universal music style that can be heard in every country of the world. It's called contemporary pop/rock.[2]

Our pastoral candidate was an enthusiastic adherent to this philosophy and so, I thought, was I. Responding to a question about what style of music he preferred for services, he remarked that the music used on Sunday in church should not be any different from the music people listen to on their car radios during the week. He went on to say that no one listens to organ music or old hymns on the radio, so why should we use that music in church? Strange as it may seem, hearing this minister of the gospel of Jesus Christ articulate the musical ideals I had come to espouse brought about an awakening in my spirit. It was as if I looked into the mirror for the first time and did not like what I saw! I began to see that this was *man's* music philosophy, not God's. Although I was unaware then of how deeply this pastor's words affected me, the Holy Spirit was bringing me to a turning point in my life. This was the beginning of the end of my CCM ministry.

Following his acceptance to the position, the new pastor expressed his excitement about our worship services and said he looked forward to working with the team. But I resigned my music ministry post shortly after he began. For reasons I did not fully understand at the time, I somehow knew that I could not fully support his music and worship philosophy. It appeared that he was going to take the service further into worldliness than I had ever imagined, and that proved to be the case. Soon afterwards, our family left the church, after which God began to reveal to me through his Word why I had become disenchanted with the ministry I had so loved.

Why I had to leave

Now I want to summarize the reasons I had to leave the CCM scene. Firstly, I could no longer accept the premises undergirding the CCM philosophy. In other words, the piles holding up the pier turned out to be rotten and crumbling. Our key premises were that music is amoral; God accepts all music styles; and no one should judge another's preference or tastes. As I dug into the Bible to prove them right, instead I saw that they were man-centred, illogical, and misrepresentations of basic biblical principles. I will cover these issues in detail later.

Secondly, when I saw what the Bible teaches about true worship and what it really means to be in the presence of God, I became sickened at the way my generation so glibly used profane and vulgar music accompanied by vulgar dress to offer up worship and praise to a holy God! And no one involved seemed to notice what we were doing. Thirdly, to preserve my marriage and to be faithful to God in all things, I needed to separate from the temptations that were ever-present in the CCM setting: the ego gratification and attraction to the female members of the worship team.

Fourthly, I saw that we were in danger of becoming the same hypocrites we accused the Traditionals of being. For example, one of our main charges against conservative church music and services was that they lacked spontaneity; they were boring and predictable. But somehow we did not notice that *our own CCM* services had become numbingly the same, week after week. The typical ex-Baptist, evangelical, community church, seeker-sensitive services were all starting to sound the same, like a group of Integrity Hosanna or Maranatha Praise clones. We managed to create a unique musical style in CCM P&W and now we have thousands of churches copying it. It's still rock but not as 'hard' as the latest secular versions. It is more laidback with a hint of the Eagles. The worship sets have fallen into a familiar (boring?) order of service. The Traditionals had some guidelines to restrain them, but Contemporaries have *no* rules, so when things become too familiar they bring in louder, jazzier and more questionable material. That is one of the curses upon CCM: the music will continually be on this slippery slope and worship leaders will be forced to accept *any* musical style, no matter how disgraceful. I had to get away from that.

We are currently members of a church where the pastors and other leaders have taken a strong stand against the use of all rock-influenced contemporary music styles in the church service. Musically speaking, I have come full circle as a Christian; back to a church with a similar musical philosophy as the one I attended when I was saved. I suppose the happy ending to my story would be to say that I am once again busily involved in the music ministry at this church. But I am not.

Consequences

There were consequences left over from my years as a Contemporary worship leader. At our new church, at first I was very critical about *every* aspect of the worship service and the leaders. I kept this criticism to myself or shared it only with Judy, but still I harboured it in my spirit. In hindsight, I can see that the

Lord was showing me that genuine worship and enthusiastic praise could still exist in a Traditional service. This reality conflicted with the views I had embraced for so many years, and I believe that conflict contributed much to my critical spirit.

I was also afraid of being involved in music ministry again. I told no one of my musical abilities and I avoided the music pastor. Because of my background and my tendencies, I felt musically unreliable to join a Traditional music programme and believed I could well become a corrupting influence on it. 'Prone to wander, Lord, I feel it!'

Instinctively I turned all music styles into my brand of pop/rock. When I played the keyboards, I unconsciously rearranged the tune into a pop/rock feel and beat. When I opened my mouth to sing, years of CCM-style vocals left me sounding too much like the rock musicians I once worked hard to imitate.

Twenty years after my conversion to Christ, I have once again asked the Lord to give me a *new song* with which to praise him, but this time I am praying that the song will be *free* from my old rock music styles.

3.
The big lie

'We can use any contemporary music style in our praise and worship services, and God will accept it.' This statement sums up the philosophy of the contemporary P&W movement. Contemporaries label as 'legalistic' any rules and regulations that would limit music choices, and instead they depend on this philosophy as their guide. Once a loyal adherent, I now believe such a philosophy is a big lie. It comes directly out of a teaching that is popular in contemporary churches: 'God accepts us as we are.'

To understand the rest of this book, it is imperative that the reader first comprehends the powerful effect this teaching of unconditional acceptance has had on the church music debate. It has completely neutralized the proper role of biblical discernment and it has done away with all guidelines. Even more importantly, we need to examine in light of the Scriptures this unspoken assumption, which is behind so many arguments used to defend CCM.

I recently received a leaflet inviting me to a local church. The soothing words assured me: 'At ... church "come as you are" means more than just casual attire. It means accepting one another without judgements or agendas. It means helping people connect to God without jumping artificial religious hurdles.' The slogan of the church is 'Church the way it was meant to be, because YOU matter to God and to us!' The church advertises its relaxing atmosphere, life messages and, of course, the contemporary music.

Is it just me, or do you also think this comes across as bait-and-switch advertising? This is a repositioned Baptist church with AWANA (a weekly children's Bible club found in fundamental and conservative Baptist churches in America), which would typically place them in the fundamental branch of the Baptists. If that is the case, then sooner or later any visitors are going to discover, much to their discomfort, that there are plenty of judgements in the Bible, and that Christ has a definite agenda for their life that has *nothing* to do with their comfort zone. Discipleship is not a self-esteem journey; growth means change, change always includes loss, and loss is always painful. You cannot keep all your old habits and pleasures. And who is to say a visitor will not consider the membership requirement of believer's baptism to be an 'artificial religious hurdle'?

The 'Come as you are, God accepts you where you are at' doctrine is closely aligned with the tolerance movement that is popular in our secular society. As you can see from the advertising example above, this is laying the foundations for some serious religious disillusionment down the road. The real test of any Christian teaching, however, is not either its short-term or long-term consequences, but whether or not it is found in the Word of God. How does this doctrine stand up to that test?

Is there any biblical truth behind 'come as you are'? It certainly reflects the biblical principle that to God 'all our righteousnesses are like filthy rags' (Isaiah 64:6). There is nothing we can do to earn our salvation; we cannot make ourselves clean enough to be acceptable to God. But does that also mean we can *stay* as we are?

John Makujina, a scholar who assiduously researched the CCM movement, has stated that,

Whereas many conservatives preached what amounts to 'Clean yourself up before you receive Christ', the Jesus movement [where CCM began] said more biblically, 'Come as you are.' The problem however was that come as you are more often meant 'remain as you are', at least as far as music, language, clothing, and social habits are concerned.[1]

The only biblical justification I have heard for this doctrine is the story in John 8 concerning the woman caught in adultery. But we cannot forget that after the Pharisees left, Jesus said to the woman, 'Neither do I condemn you; go and *sin no more.*' Jesus did not accept her as she was — he commanded her to change. Neither does Jesus accept us as *we* are. When we become his disciples, he expects us to sin no more, to show a change in our affections from idols to him, and for us to turn from the lusts of the world and love him.

There is no biblical proof of a God who accepts anyone for 'who he is'. God is not interested in our self-esteem or our filthy rags. Examine the evidence and judge for yourself. We know that God is a holy God who hates sin (the Ten Commandments of Exodus 20:1-17; Proverbs 6:16; Zechariah 8:17; Malachi 2:16). We also know that God extends his mercy to repentant sinners (2 Chronicles 7:14; Ezekiel 18:21-22; Jeremiah 18:8; 2 Peter 3:9). To be accepted by God, we must come through Jesus Christ (John 14:6). Jesus did not accept a sinner's sin. He preached repentance from sin to everyone, not just to the Pharisees.

Romans 8:29 implies that we do not remain as we are. God is undertaking the amazing process of conforming us to the image of Christ. This is a definite movement away from worldliness and towards holiness. 1 Corinthians 6:9-10 and the entire book of 1 John also make it clear that we cannot remain in our sinful practices and still hope to gain acceptance from God.

On the contrary, 1 Peter 2:11 warns us to 'abstain from fleshly lusts which war against the soul'.

The New Testament clearly teaches that genuine conversion produces a changed — and changing — life. The metamorphosis begins on the inside with a 'new heart' and 'a new spirit' (Ezekiel 36:26), and as we feed on God's Word and offer our very lives to him rather than to the world, our minds are renewed in such a way that we 'are being transformed into the same image'— the image of Christ (Romans 8:29; 2 Corinthians 3:18). 'Do not be conformed to this world, but be transformed by the renewing of your mind' is the command from Romans 12:2. The first part of that command literally means: 'Do not fashion yourself according to the pattern of the current age.'

The honest 'seeker' must conclude that this 'come as you are' teaching of God's unconditional acceptance is at best misleading. We cannot come to God just as we are, with our sin unconfessed or ignored or draped all over us, and still expect his acceptance. We cannot drag our favourite worldly music, dress and language into the church, and expect a blessing! That is wishful thinking with no basis in Scripture. Nor would we want 'unchurched seekers' to believe they can hang on to their sins and still be accepted by God. But that is the implied message from many pulpits and youth leaders. Seeker-sensitive pastors are prone to emphasize God's mercy and acceptance, and to downplay God's judgement so as not to offend the seeker.

Acceptance doctrine is so pervasive in some fellowships that Christians are no longer allowed to question another Christian's behaviour or personal preferences. If you confront another in love, you will be accused of judging them. If you dare quote chapter and verse from the Bible, you will be called a Pharisee. If a church has any practices that step on the toes of anyone's personal preferences, then it is considered to be a legalistic church.

If God accepts me as I am, then surely he accepts my personal preferences in worship style. If my heart is in the right place, who has the right to tell me I should be in church every Sunday? God knows I'm not perfect and he still loves me, so how can anyone else hold me accountable for my actions? This type of thinking imitates the world's attitude of tolerance, which demands that no one can judge anyone else's lifestyle or behaviour because all lifestyles are equal and everyone has a right to be left alone to their own devices. Please understand that I am *not* advocating the law over grace, or external rules over internal obedience. I just want to emphasize how far the pendulum has swung from the legalism of the 1970s to the licence of the new millennium.

In this new Church of Acceptance, showing tolerance for worldly affections and behaviours is far more important than exercising biblical discernment. A person is simply not allowed to question another's personal preference, and if he does, then he must produce a *specific* Bible verse to back it up. (But as we will discover throughout this book, the Contemporary often does not hold himself to that same biblical standard to defend his own arguments.) In this thoroughly biased atmosphere, it is easy to see why a Traditional is afraid to speak out about music styles. It is also apparent why CCM styles have been accepted so easily by so many with no discernment about the negative effects.

'Not everyone who says to me, "Lord, Lord", shall enter the kingdom of heaven, but he who does the will of my Father in heaven' (Matthew 7:21). *This is the truth.* 'God accepts you where you are, no matter what.' *This is the big lie.*

I contend that the wholesale embracing of CCM by many churches is a direct consequence of our failure to confront and refute 'acceptance' teaching. Perhaps we wanted to avoid any hint of being labelled as 'legalists'. We have traded biblical discernment for tolerance of all forms of worldliness, so why should it come as any surprise that 'anything goes' with music in church? CCM's use in worship has been firmly established through the 'mother' lie of acceptance doctrine and further justified by several 'baby' lies and half-truths, which shall be discussed later. This false teaching has opened the doors of our churches to the spirits of immorality, divisiveness and deception.

A spirit of immorality

One of Satan's favourite methods of compromise is to break down standards of Christian modesty and convince us to be more 'open' about our sexuality. This is the same attack he uses with great success on unbelievers, keeping them in bondage to their immorality. His tools of the trade include sensual music, sensual performers, sexual images, alcohol and drugs. Can Satan's ploy work on Christians too? It can and it does.

When we brought rock music (and all its musical cousins) into the church service, we invited along with it a spirit of immorality with which that music is *unavoidably* associated. It wasn't obvious at first. We didn't use hard rock; instead we used more acceptable, watered-down forms of it: soft rock, pop/rock, country rock and easy listening jazz styles. These styles supported the warm and fuzzy, falling-in-love-with-God feelings we wanted to have in worship. They were less edgy but still contained the underlying rock beat that undeniably appeals to our flesh and reminds us of the world's favourite music.

Despite all our efforts to restrain this musical beast, the saints of God are being seduced by CCM styles. These styles are capable of corrupting the morals of *any* Christian, no matter how strong they think they are. What are the signs of a spirit of immorality in our churches? We will cover this in chapter 6, 'Seducing the saints'.

A spirit of divisiveness

Let me sum up a Contemporary's typical attitude towards any who oppose the use of CCM in the church. 'We need to pray for these poor, tradition-bound people who just don't understand the heart of worship. They are standing in the way of what God wants to do.' I am not making this up — I once had the same attitude.

This condescending attitude leads to a spirit of divisiveness, and I believe it has infected many worship leaders today as it did me. These leaders actually believe that God is trying to do something special through their use of whatever new music styles they feel God leads them to use. Anyone who stands in their way will be labelled a legalistic Pharisee, or will be put on the defensive with some of the arguments you will read more about later in this book.

The Contemporary's attitude signals that anyone who resists should either go along with the programme and accept CCM, or find another church. This spirit has affected even pastors. I will show how this divisive spirit is a direct result of the Contemporary's attitude, how it makes a Traditional feel powerless to respond and often feel compelled to leave the church. We will address this issue in chapter 7, 'Splitting churches'.

A spirit of deception

It all goes back to the big lie that 'God accepts me as I am; therefore he accepts my music.' Out of that belief has sprung several popular arguments used by Contemporaries to introduce CCM into a church and to justify its continued use. The arguments may sound perfectly reasonable and logical and are easy for many Christians to swallow whole — especially if they're already convinced that exercising discernment about music means being judgemental. But beneath these arguments is a spirit of deception at work that dulls our ability to discern the difference between the proper and the profane.

We will spend several chapters discussing such popular arguments as:

- It's all just a matter of personal preference and taste.
- We're just trying to reach the unchurched.
- Music is amoral.
- God made music — isn't all music inherently good?
- Show me where the Bible says that rock music is evil.
- Doesn't the Bible teach it's OK to use different music styles to reach people?
- A blended service will please everyone.
- It's the heart of worship that really matters, not the music.
- Didn't Martin Luther and the Wesleys use contemporary music in church?
- CCM is easier to sing than hymns.
- Isn't God using CCM to save and disciple teens?

We will learn why these arguments are wrong or misleading. I am aware some CCM defenders are demanding that anyone who challenges CCM arguments must provide them with specific and clear reasons from God's Word to support their objection. I find that demand somewhat ironic since most Contemporaries I know or have read do not adhere to this same practice; but I accept the challenge. Wherever possible, I will give chapter and verse of the Bible to back up my convictions.

A serious charge

Why single out CCM for such intense scrutiny? Can't these spirits and attitudes infiltrate the church through other means? Yes, they can. But only music has been placed in such a position of great power and authority in so many churches today. The music ministry has taken over our worship services. CCM styles are promoted up front on the platform, right there before us every time we assemble, dominating the hour or so we spend together. Simply by its unchallenged presence in the service, CCM receives the implicit stamp of approval from the church leadership, whether or not that is what they intend. We are all led to believe there is nothing wrong with CCM in church. On the contrary, we probably think we did something good for God when we made the change from that old, boring traditional music.

Many believers think contemporary music is the only way they can truly praise and worship the Lord. (You don't agree? Then I suggest you take their music away from them and watch their reaction!) Some pastors believe CCM is the most important means of making their services more relevant and 'user-friendly' to the all-important unchurched. Popular books about marketing the church magnify the importance of contemporary music, and these books have influenced pastors and music ministers.

How important has CCM become in churches? When asked what one thing he would do differently if he could start his church all over again, here is what Rick Warren (the well-known pastor of Saddleback Community Church in California, USA, mentioned earlier) had to say:

> From the first day of the new church I'd put more energy and money into a first-class music ministry that matched our target. In the first years of Saddleback, I made the mistake of underestimating the power of music so I minimized the use of music in our services. I regret that now.[2]

I chose to quote Pastor Warren because his book is an indispensable guide for many a fundamental or evangelical pastor who wants his church to grow by becoming more contemporary and relevant to unbelievers. His book has spawned a worldwide ministry. According to the Purpose Driven Church web site (www.purposedriven.com), over 200,000 people have been trained on his methodology and thousands of churches are implementing PDC methods. Pastor Warren wrote a chapter about the importance of using CCM to reach people and, having read the book, I am familiar with his music philosophy.

Music sets the atmosphere of the church service, communicates doctrine through singing, and expresses our view of what God is like. Warren further states:

> The style of music you choose to use in your service will be one of the most critical (and controversial) decisions you make in the life of your church. It may also be *the* most influential factor in determining who your church reaches for Christ and whether or not your church grows.[3]

Pastor Warren's quotes demonstrate how unquestionably important CCM has become as the key to success for the contemporary church. But he gives *no* biblical basis for attributing such a lofty status to CCM — only his opinion. In contrast, I will show how giving such a prominent position to CCM may very well be *un*scriptural. Our acceptance of CCM into worship services has hurt an entire generation of older Christians, has led to church splits, and has created a breeding ground for immorality, selfishness and divisive attitudes in younger generations.

These charges are a hard pill to swallow for any leader who has happily embraced CCM. No one knows this better than me. I had to admit that I too was deceived by my own lusts and selfishness. I was taken in by the big lie and its arguments, and the sinful spirits mentioned above hounded me. My devotion to CCM caused division in my marriage, confusion in my family and interfered with my personal relationship with Jesus.

No matter how hard I tried, my music ministry did not seem to bear good fruit in people's lives by producing holiness and obedience. Some who are unfamiliar with my ministry will jump to the conclusion that the problem was all mine, that I was simply not cut out for this and therefore I cannot indict the contemporary P&W movement for my own failure. However, at one time, many Contemporaries told me I was 'gifted by God' to lead praise and worship. I received strong affirmations of this from many pastors, denominational leaders, other musicians and the members of the congregations I served. How could one so 'gifted' fail?

But I had to flee from CCM's corrupting influence on my life. Coming out of CCM was (and continues to be) a very humbling and painful experience for me, a person who was full of pride in the area of music ministry. This is a very difficult book for me to write. I hate being wrong about *anything* I do for the Lord! All those hours spent working on music for him — were they wasted? Were they less effective than they could have been? I grieve when I let down my Lord and Saviour. I am hurt when I realize the effects on his church. But perhaps my experience can either prevent some from falling into or help others escape from the CCM trap.

What *is* acceptable worship to God?

In his introduction to a commentary on Psalms, Matthew Henry said:

> It is absolutely necessary to the acceptance of our devotions that we be righteous before God (for it is only the prayer of the upright that is his delight), and therefore that we be right in our notions of blessedness and in our choice of the way that leads to it.[4]

David's definition of acceptable worship in Psalm 51:15-17 seems particularly apt:

O Lord, open my lips,
And my mouth shall show forth your praise.
For you do not desire sacrifice, or else I would give it;
You do not delight in burnt offering.
The sacrifices of God are a broken spirit,
A broken and a contrite heart—
These, O God, you will not despise.

How then shall we worship together?

We will examine the subject of worship in depth in the next chapter, titled 'What is the *true* heart of worship?' After a discussion of the problems caused by the use of CCM in the church, I will call other Contemporaries to join me in a bold movement of reformation.

- Let's remove the worldly CCM styles and influences from our services.
- Let's return to traditional and conservative music styles in our services.

At this point, I can almost hear the Contemporary groaning out loud, 'I will never ever go back to that stuffy, dead service!' Someone is probably making a bumper sticker right now that says, 'You can have my CCM when you pry it from my cold, dead fingers!'[5] Years of CCM propaganda may have convinced him or her that the contemporary service is the only way to experience genuine, spontaneous and diverse worship, and therefore anything associated with conservative services is fake and dead worship. This is exactly how I first felt when we left a contemporary-style church service to return to a conservative church service.

But I have good news for the Contemporaries who are courageous enough to consider such a reformation. You *can* have a Spirit-filled, exciting, 'close-encounter-with-God' worship service *without* CCM styles. Without a praise band. With good old hymns and non-rock contemporary songs. God inhabits the praise of his people without the presence of controversial music styles and performances that closely imitate the world's music system. I know this is true because my church has that kind of worship service.

For those who doubt you can ever go back, we will take a look at how my local church worships God *without* the use of CCM styles. We are a diverse church with several Hispanic families, and together we experience genuine and spontaneous worship *without* CCM or the need to use culturally correct music styles. To those who would like to pursue musical reform, I will also offer some advice on choosing appropriate music for our worship and praise to God.

4.
What is the *true* 'heart of worship'?

Occasionally I participate in a worship leaders' online forum, which works like a bulletin board. Someone posts a question and then others reply in a message thread. The subjects are about music and worship issues in the church, and it is where I first heard of the wonderful-sounding 'heart of worship' concept.

I have heard various explanations from members of the forum of what this is supposed to mean. I believe it originates in the truth that God looks at the inward man (the heart), but when I saw how it was actually applied by its adherents, I discerned more deception at work. What sounds 'holy' can be twisted into another false justification for CCM.

This concept was typically invoked in the forum as a defensive response when anyone questioned the appropriateness of CCM use in church services. 'Do some members of the church question your choice of music?' 'They just do not understand the "heart of worship".' 'Do you have a problem with the dress style of the ladies on your worship team?' 'You do not need rules; it's the "heart of worship" that matters.' 'If I like punk music, does God still accept me?' 'The style doesn't matter, it's the "heart of worship" that matters.' I did not make up these questions and answers; they are representative of what is debated in the forum.

I am not saying that the heart is less important than the 'form' of worship. Neither do I doubt the sincerity of Contemporaries in this matter. On the contrary, I agree that the attitude of the heart *is* the most important factor! Where we differ is in our definition of the *true* heart of worship. Do Contemporaries speak biblically when they talk about the 'heart of worship'? I have examined a wide variety of 'Worship Philosophy' statements from churches that use CCM in their worship services, and I have discussed this online with other Contemporary worship leaders. If space and time permitted, I would reveal dozens of statements that all sound essentially the same. In some, the Bible is acknowledged but not followed. In others, the Bible is used as a guideline for *every* area *except* the music style. In all, the writers make statements that are unsupported by biblical texts yet popular across the Contemporary spectrum.

I fear that in the vast majority of Contemporary churches (and also in some Traditional churches), our worship practices have strayed far away from the *true* biblical heart of worship because we have failed to base our practices firmly on the Word of God and instead built the foundation on the needs of man. Why should we fear this? Because how could we possibly expect God to accept our worship and bless us, if we define worship in *any other fashion than what his Word requires?* Were humans given a choice of *how* to worship God? Can the pottery choose *how* to respond to the Potter's touch? Would God be angry with us if we use *ourselves* as the measure of how to worship him, rather than his Word?

Obviously the next question we have to ask ourselves is this: Does God in his Word give *any* clear direction for the manner in which he is to be worshipped? The answer is: 'Yes, he does!' When I went through this study, God changed for ever my casual, 'come as you are' attitude about worship services! To the worship leaders and pastors reading this book, I ask you now to accept the challenge of discovering the truth about worship.

Different meanings

Before we can come together on this matter, we first have to understand that the Contemporary and the Traditional are speaking different languages. The very meaning of the word *worship* has been changed by Contemporaries to suit CCM philosophies. It no longer refers to the biblical practice of bowing in reverence and humility before a holy God. The word itself has been expanded beyond this basic meaning to include all the forms used for worship: any style of music played by any musician, dancing, drama and art. It can mean the service itself, and anything that occurs within it.

This kind of re-definition is a major cause for concern for me, and should alarm every believer. The Word of God has specific inspired and inerrant meanings in the original languages. We must be careful not to corrupt the words of Scripture by changing or expanding their meanings to suit our latest tastes, fashions or styles. The Lord Jesus also made it clear that we will be held accountable for all our words (Matthew 12:36-37). What does the word 'worship' really mean? How can we discover the true 'heart' and be faithful to the Bible? God has given us clear definitions.

Biblical worship

Let's start with the very meaning of biblical worship. Worship is an English word. According to *Webster's New World College Dictionary*, 4th edition, worship means 'reverence or devotion for a deity; religious homage or veneration'. The word combines two Old English words with German origins: worth (to honour) and –ship (to create). When English-speaking people worship God, we literally *create honour* to God with our actions and words. Worship has also been described as 'ascribing (assigning, attributing) honour to' God.

The word 'worship' was chosen by the translators because it is as close as we have in our English language to the Hebrew and Greek words. But as you will see next, this word alone simply cannot convey the totality of what God is saying when we are told to worship him. I believe this lack of biblical knowledge contributes to our acceptance of worship practices that are not acceptable to God. Without this knowledge to give us boundaries, we devise too easily our own ideas about how to worship God. That is why every Christian should learn to use a Hebrew and Greek lexicon such as *Strong's Concordance*. With all the great Bible study books and software, we do not have to become Greek or Hebrew scholars to gain more insight into the words of God.

In the Old Testament, the Hebrew word translated as 'worship' is *shachah*, which *Strong's Concordance* defines as 'to depress, to prostrate (especially in homage to royalty or God); to bow oneself down, to crouch, to fall down flat, to humbly beseech'. In the New Testament, the Greek word translated most commonly as 'worship' is *proskuneo*, which means 'to kiss like a dog licking his master's hand; to fawn or to crouch; to prostrate oneself in homage'.

In Middle Eastern societies, especially Persia, which had exerted much influence over the region, the ancient mode of greeting one another was determined by rank. Zodhiates vividly describes the cultural meaning of *proskuneo*:

> Persons of equal rank kissed each other on the lips. When the difference of rank was slight, they kissed each other on the cheek. When one was much inferior, he fell upon

his knees and touched his forehead to the ground or pros-
trated himself, throwing kisses at the same time towards
the superior.

It is this latter mode of salutation that Greek writers
expressed by *proskuneo*. In the NT, generally, to do
reverence or homage to someone, usually by kneeling or
prostrating oneself in reverence, homage.[1]

When we approach God in worship, is our attitude in keeping with these definitions? The thought that we are to be like
dogs subservient to their master is quite repulsive to a Contemporary, who prefers to keep his or her dignity and self-esteem
intact while worshipping. Let's face it — we would rather
undertake activities that lift *ourselves* up, than wait upon God
to do the lifting. But Peter wrote in his first epistle, 'Humble
yourselves under the mighty hand of God, that he may exalt
you in due time' (1 Peter 5:6).

What about the physical position described so vividly above?
Should we literally prostrate ourselves whenever we worship
God, just as our spiritual forefathers did? We may recoil from
that thought as we consider the images on our television sets of
Muslims, for example, performing their prayer ritual, which includes an act of prostration that at least in its form fits the meaning of worship. But God sees our hearts; he is not fooled by the
form of prostration, he desires a broken and penitent heart that
is committed to him.

What about the New Testament believers who are privileged
to live in this 'age of grace'? We no longer worship according to
prescribed rituals, but we must still worship God 'in spirit and
truth' (John 4:24). When Satan tempted him (Matthew 4:8-
10), Jesus clarified what he meant by worshipping in *truth*: 'It is
written.' He quoted the Old Testament law to Satan: 'You shall
fear the LORD your God and serve him' (Deuteronomy 6:13).
Our worship must be based on truth as 'it is written', not on our

experience, our feelings, the felt needs of the consumer, or our man-centred version of the truth.

What about worshipping God in *spirit?* According to Barnes,

> As he is such a spirit, he dwells not in temples made with hands (Acts 7:48), neither is worshipped with men's hands as though he needed anything, seeing he giveth to all life, and breath, and all things, Acts 17:25. *A pure, a holy, a spiritual worship, therefore, is such as he seeks* — the offering of the soul rather than the formal offering of the body — *the homage of the heart* rather than that of the lips (emphasis added).[2]

How can we be sure to worship God in both spirit and truth at the same time? In his *Commentary* Adam Clarke said,

> A man worships God in spirit, when, under the influence of the Holy Ghost, he brings all his affections, appetites, and desires to the throne of God; and he worships him in truth, when *every* purpose and passion of his heart, and when *every* act of his religious worship, is guided and regulated by the word of God.

Complete submission

Is it clear now what the 'heart of worship' truly is? When we approach God, the attitude of our hearts must be one of complete submission. We have nothing to offer God except our total devotion and obedience. We must examine our own worship service in light of the true meaning of worship. Does anything occur in that service that does not fit the biblical meaning?

When we worship we must be very careful not to exalt our feelings over truth, as I did on more than one occasion. 'Humble Thyself in the Sight of the Lord', a popular CCM worship song, was one of my favourites. I used this song to 'usher people into the presence of God' (a standard line of the Contemporary worship leader). The lyrics are taken from James 4:10.

Humble Thyself in the Sight of the Lord,
And He will lift you up, *higher and higher*
(emphasis added).[3]

In the main translations James 4:10 does not include the phrase 'higher and higher'. Whatever the reason it was added by the song writer, I believe this aptly illustrates a major problem with the Contemporary's notion of worship: that God wants to affirm us through worship, to make us feel good about ourselves with the result that we will have this grand experience of feeling higher and higher.

In my own experience, I noticed that we Contemporaries preferred to raise our faces and hands up to God, and called that worship. But as we saw earlier in this chapter, worship is *not* looking up and feeling good, it is bowing down and feeling lowly. If we try to add any other experience to worship, we have left the true meaning and are travelling into experiential territory where man is the judge of what is right and wrong. I thought back to when I first changed my personal worship style from bowing my head to looking up. I was influenced by charismatics praying in one of our city-wide prayer meetings. I remember the good feeling it gave me that I was for the first time a participant in worship *with* God, not some lowly worm who had to prostrate myself. I felt better about myself!

It is certainly biblical to feel happy in Jesus but I now realize that a good personal feeling is *not* part of biblical worship. When we try to feel an experience of affirmation from worship, we are not worshipping God. We are worshipping our own egos. If we are to be lifted up by God, we simply cannot create that experience through the pseudo style of worship we practise as Contemporaries. We must pay attention to what Scripture teaches.

One lesson I learned from my study was that I cannot bring any of my old sinful desires and practices into worship to a holy God and expect him to accept them! I am now convinced that God will not accept our worship when it is offered with music styles that are also used by pagans for their immoral practices. If I am wrong, why was he so harsh in judging Israel when they sacrificed to him using the pagan high places and rituals? He is a jealous God. If you grasp this principle alone, it will change for ever the way you lead a worship service.

Another lesson I drew from my study is that our worship must also contain a sense of the *fear* of God, not just the comfortable 'Abba Father' feeling that many Contemporaries seem to prefer. I had lost that fear in my CCM worship practice; it was replaced by a much more comfortable feeling that I was doing something good for God and he would bless me. I relegated *fear of God* to the Old Testament and if someone told me I should be worshipping in fear, I considered they were being legalistic. I have been to many other CCM worship services and have not seen this fear manifested by anyone — ever. The feelings we sought and produced in people were 180 degrees from fear; our worship made us feel *closer to God, accepted for who we are!*

Sense of fear

We can now see that true worship must produce a sense of fear in the worshipper towards the *worshipped*. Do not be afraid (no pun intended) to embrace the word *fear*. The baby boomers banned *fear* from church because it conflicted with our self-esteem and our acceptance doctrine, but it is still there in the Bible. If you think the fear of God ceased after the book of Malachi was completed to end the Old Testament, then why did Peter command us to 'fear God' (1 Peter 2:17)? You may be thinking that what he *really* meant there was to *respect* God; I too have often heard that translation from pastors and Christian counsellors. But the Greek word is *phobos;* it means to frighten; to be alarmed; to be in awe of; to revere; to be sore afraid; to fear exceedingly (*Strong's Concordance*). Why would these pastors and counsellors change the meaning to something softer and easier? Was it to support the self-esteem of their flock?

Commenting on 1 Peter 2:17, Barnes said, 'A holy veneration or fear is always an elementary principle of religion. It is the fear not so much of punishment as of his disapprobation [disapproval]; not so much the dread of suffering as the dread of doing wrong.' See also Colossians 3:22. In 1 John 4:18 (which states 'there is no fear in love'), John was not reversing what Peter and Paul said. Some Contemporaries have misinterpreted this passage to justify their opinion that we are no longer to have any fear of God as part of our relationship with him. But in the context, John is comforting believers who still feared eternal punishment. He tells them that perfect love will give us boldness, not fear, in the day of judgement.

Misunderstanding leads to error

Misunderstanding the biblical meaning of the heart of worship leads to error. Answers to questions in the online forum *rarely* included the Word of God. Instead, human opinions were expressed over and over again. Some erroneous statements were repeated again and again until they appeared to be truthful.

Here is one example of a recent exchange.

Q. I recently became a Christian but I still like to listen to secular punk music. Do I need to give it up?

A. God cares more about the heart of worship, not the style of your music. There is a lot of good Christian punk out there.

On the contrary, God *does* care about the style of music too. Punk music is the ultimate statement of musical rebellion. Changing the words and the artists and calling it Christian will never sanctify it. It has no place in a new Christian's life. I fear this young man will continue in bondage to his old sinful habits as he listens to Christian punk, encouraged by a worship leader. Any time we misunderstand a biblical principle, we lead others and ourselves into error and sin. In this case, a new Christian was deceived into thinking that he can hold on to some of his old styles. We need to have the courage to rebuke this kind of theology wherever we find it.

Another disturbing trend on the forum was the negative reaction from fellow worship leaders whenever the Word of God was introduced into a discussion. Along with a few others, I regularly included Scripture in my postings. Yet we would often receive a reply that included the words 'Pharisee' or 'legalistic'. And someone would undoubtedly warn us that in worship the heart is more important than the mind. Be wary of any Christian who reacts negatively to Scripture. And make sure *you* rightly divide the Word of God. Do not use it out of context or to purposely hurt someone. Simply present it.

The true heart of worship is the heart that bows before God and submits to his Word, no more and no less. This is the attitude of the writer of Hebrews: 'Let us have grace, by which we may serve God acceptably with reverence and godly fear. For our God is a consuming fire' (Hebrews 12:28-29). When a worship leader is confronted with this, he or she will never be the same again! This knowledge will permeate their musical preferences and they will be so very careful when choosing music to usher in the worship of the holy God. That is what happened to me, and God used this knowledge to open my eyes to see the deception at work. Once we learn the truth about biblical worship, we should no longer stand for the errors and misuses occurring in churches that have embraced CCM.

Even some CCM artists realize that their songs, their performances and their lifestyles are not reflecting the true heart of worship. Jerry Williams, the leader of the Christian rock group Harvest, wrote a song in the early 1990s called 'What Are You Singing For?' His lyrics criticized strongly those CCM artists who were crossing over to pop music and watering down the message of the cross of Christ. He accused them of being more concerned about the performance and their own appearance and fame, than about the souls of the listeners and the glory of God.

Steve Camp, one of the early leaders of Christian rock and a CCM recording artist, became so offended by the CCM industry that he published on the Internet his 107 theses calling CCM artists to reformation of their worldly business practices and compromise. He wrote:

Music is a powerful tool from the Lord Jesus to his church intended for worship, praise, encouragement, edification, evangelism, teaching, and admonishing. And exhorting God's people to holiness — with always our chief aim 'to glorify God and worship Him forever'. But beloved, the serpentine foe of compromise has invaded the camp through years of specious living, skewed doctrine and most recently secular ownership of Christian music ministries.[4]

I close this chapter with an astounding confession from Matt Redman, a leading contemporary worship leader, in his song 'The Heart of Worship':

> When the music fades, all is stripped away, and I simply come,
> Longing just to bring, something that's of worth that will bless Your heart.
> I'll bring You more than a song, for a song itself is not what You have required,
> You search much deeper within through the way things appear.
> You're looking into my heart.
>
> I'm coming back to the heart of worship,
> And it's all about You, Jesus,
> I'm sorry Lord for the thing I've made it,
> When it's all about You, all about You, Jesus.[5]

5.
I want my MTV!

'We are trying to reach the unchurched.' This is a common excuse you will hear for using CCM in church services.

John MacArthur warned us that the rush to make churches user-friendly '... has become an excuse for importing worldly amusements into the church in an attempt to try to attract non-Christian "seekers" or "unchurched Harrys" by appealing to their fleshly interests'.[1] In his commentary on the book of Acts, MacArthur stated that 'making the Lord the object of ministry obviates the need for compromise. Those whose goal is ministering to people will be tempted to compromise to achieve that end.' Was he right about that!

However, the seeker was not the *only* one whose fleshly interests were being indulged. It is time to expose the hypocrisy of those church leaders who justify CCM by claiming they use it for evangelistic purposes in their seeker services. Nonsense! The truth is, these churches use it in their services for the 'saints' as well. One of the major problems with seeker-oriented music is that it must not only 'sink' to appeal to man's fallen nature, but is also bound to stir up the believer's sinful nature, his 'flesh', as Paul called it. At the seeker-sensitive churches we attended, the music was ostensibly designed for the unchurched but that excuse was really just a smoke screen obscuring our *real* reason for bringing CCM into the service. The bottom line was that we simply wanted to use *our* music in the church, not what we perceived as our parents' or grandparents' music. We have the same self-centred, self-indulgent spirit of the 1960s and 1970s but now it has been given a veneer of Christian dedication.

I call this the 'I want my MTV!' attitude. That phrase was a popular advertising slogan promoting MTV in the 1980s. The advertising hook was diabolically clever. It really means: 'I want to listen to *my* music whenever *I* feel like it and don't you tell me that I can't.' This is the spirit of self-indulgence, not the Spirit of God. We brought this spirit into church with our music masquerading as a tool for better evangelism.

In 1996, Al Mohler Jr, President of the Southern Baptist Seminary, wrote:

> The ubiquitous culture of consumerism and materialism has seduced many evangelicals into a ministry mode driven by marketing rather than mission. To an ever greater extent, evangelicals are accommodating themselves to moral compromise in the name of lifestyle and choice. Authentic biblical worship is often supplanted by the entertainment culture as issues of performance and taste displace the simplicity and God-centeredness of true worship. Our churches are worldly in lifestyle, worship, and piety. We have seen the worship of God too often made into a human-centered entertainment event.[2]

A. W. Tozer, a wise pastor, saw the problem over fifty years ago. He wrote in 1948:

> I wonder if there was ever a time when true spiritual worship was at a lower ebb. To great sections of the church the art of worship has been lost entirely, and in its place has come that strange and foreign thing called the

'program'. This word has been borrowed from the stage and applied with sad wisdom to the type of public service which now passes for worship among us.[3]

I first encountered the self-indulgent, entertainment-minded attitude described by these men when I was a worship leader at a church in Colorado. The underlying attitude revealed itself whenever we debated the place of contemporary music in a worship service. It was not lying there on the surface where it may have been easier to spot. It was well hidden beneath the standard arguments, and it usually surfaced only after those arguments had been successfully refuted. Sometimes this attitude manifested itself in a common defensive response from a Contemporary, the accusation that anyone disputing their position was a hypocrite and a Pharisee.

The Contemporary is always the last to recognize this attitude in himself. There is often no sense at all that such a spirit is at work. Even though the Holy Spirit was prompting me to confront this spirit for several years, I was in denial. I thought I had all the right motives for what I was doing musically. I was doing it for God, not for me! The thought that my own selfish attitude could possibly be involved was hard to accept, because it would 'knock the legs out' from under my concept of ministry.

The baby boomers

The self-indulgent spirit entered the church with the baby boomers. The urge to change church music coincided with our rise to church leadership positions in the mid-1980s. The pastors leading the seeker-sensitive movement are baby boomers. I am a baby boomer who grew to maturity in the mid-1970s.

The '70s boomer group has sometimes been dubbed the 'Me' generation and now we are bringing our pervasive 'Me-ness' into church leadership and practice. If we are not careful to die to ourselves constantly and live by the Spirit, we can become 'Christian narcissists' who want Jesus to help us reach our full potential. This besetting sin of our generation will seep into every aspect of church life and ministry. It is already reflected in our music styles, which are the same styles used by the secular narcissists to glorify self-love and sensuality.

We think we worship the true God but our self-centred attitude interferes, stealing some of the attention away from him, so that our worship becomes less God-centred and more people-centred. Notice how the authors of the Cambridge Declaration of the Alliance of Confessing Evangelicals framed the problem:

> The loss of God's centrality in the life of today's church is common and lamentable. It is this loss that allows us to transform worship into entertainment, gospel preaching into marketing, believing into technique, being good into feeling good about ourselves, and faithfulness into being successful. As a result, God, Christ and the Bible have come to mean too little to us and rest too inconsequentially upon us.
>
> We deny that we can properly glorify God if our worship is confused with entertainment, if we neglect either Law or Gospel in our preaching, or if self-improvement, self-esteem or self-fulfilment are allowed to become alternatives to the gospel.[4]

In his Sunday morning sermon on 21 October 2001, Craig Scott, the senior pastor of Woodside Baptist Church in Denver, Colorado, preached that we must always remember that *God* is our audience for ministry; not ourselves and not the congregation. Keeping the focus on God will affect every choice we make for ministry, including the music we choose and the way we perform it. If ever there was a generation of Christians who need to hear and learn that truth, it is mine.

The victims

To close this chapter, I would like to point out that there have been 'victims' of our self-centred, callous attitude. Our adoption of CCM for the church service has alienated, hurt and even chased away some of our precious elder Christians and other committed believers. We witnessed the fulfilment of what MacArthur went on to say:

> The obvious fallout of this pre-occupation with the unchurched is a corresponding de-emphasis on those who are the true church. The spiritual needs of believers are often neglected to the hurt of the body.[5]

To this I would add that we have also become preoccupied with perfecting a music ministry that strokes the ego and fulfils the desires of carnal believers, to the detriment of the more serious disciples in our midst.

To the elder members in our churches and those younger who share their views on church music, I hope you can understand now what motivated us to throw away the hymns and spiritual songs that you and countless generations of Christians cherished. In our desire to gratify our fleshly lusts, we rebelled against your music, just like our generation had done with secular music since the 1960s. But in the face of your objections, we condescendingly swept your views out of consideration,

portrayed our new music as evidence of greater spiritual aware-
ness on our part, and made you appear, and perhaps feel, out
of touch and out of date. I repent of my generation's foolishness and ask for your forgiveness.

But God is not mocked. Whatever we sow, we shall also
reap. My Christian generation is undergoing severe disciplines
allowed by God, with terrible consequences such as an appal-
ling divorce rate, absentee fathers, teenagers who care more
about the world than about holy living, and hurting, broken
families. God, have mercy on us.

6.
Seducing the saints

CCM embraces many different contemporary music styles with a heavily syncopated beat, such as soft rock, smooth jazz, rap and pop/rock, but the father of them all is rock and roll. Rock and roll is a musical style that was created for immoral purposes by immoral men, and has always been used by the world to express its immoral attitudes in song. You have probably heard this before but it is worth repeating here. The name 'rock and roll' originated from a slang phrase for having sex. Rock music is the overwhelming preference of the sexually immoral, of wild partiers, of the strip joints, of drunks, and of drug abusers.

Why do you think they all prefer this style to others? The answer should be obvious to any who know rock music. Be honest with yourself as I have. We prefer it because we like the beat, the driving rhythms. Rock music and its offspring have the power to make our flesh and our minds *do something*. That 'something' must be conducive to the list of immoral behaviours we have just noted, or else these people would simply not use rock music. They would find something else to suit their fleshly desires.

It should be no surprise then that this music, which emphasizes sensuality and rebellion, often gives rise to other behaviour that evidences a spirit of immorality. But as a CCM leader, I fought against anyone who dared to suggest this was happening. One of my favourite comebacks was: 'Well, I don't see any orgies breaking out during the worship set!' Like other Contemporaries, I was blind to the subtle sexual influences creeping into my worship teams and unwilling to admit that my worship music could possibly be tainted by sex. If it was, I honestly could not have used it to usher people into the presence of a holy God.

To satisfy any nagging doubts in our consciences, we also had to deny the corrupting power of the music itself. How did we do that? We deceived ourselves into believing that all music is amoral. All we had to do was separate the rock music from the immoral words, musicians and environment, and it would be 'safe' for Christians. Once we were taken in by that clever, relativistic argument, the floodgates were opened and we could enjoy the music guilt-free. We could use our rock music for the glory of God.

I now believe that we have been *completely* deceived by that argument. We are allowing Satan a wide-open door to seduce the saints, to keep our attention on what feels good to us, and to keep us walking in the flesh not walking by the Spirit. Satan wants to diminish what God says is appropriate, and he has tricked us into public practices that used to be considered shameful. If he can get us to do this in our worship service, of all places, he has won, hasn't he? Like Israel, aren't we then guilty of mixing true worship with idolatrous practices?

Of course, we don't *think* we are being immoral or idolatrous. It's all about how we *feel*. We believe we can handle rock music safely and clean it up, because we are saved and we ask God to use it. Wrong! We cannot separate the style of music from its immoral associations. Rock music inevitably corrupts Christians. Look at what Paul says in Ephesians.

Ephesians 2:3: '...we all once conducted ourselves in the lusts of our flesh, fulfilling the desires of the flesh and of the mind, and were by nature children of wrath, just as the other'.

Ephesians 4:22-24: 'that you put off, concerning your former conduct, the old man which grows corrupt according to the deceitful lusts, and be renewed in the spirit of your mind; and that you put on the new man which was created according to God, in true righteousness and holiness'.

Christians still have a sinful nature (the old man) that constantly competes against our new Spirit-filled nature. Rock music is an example of a former conduct that fulfils the desires of the flesh and mind, and feeds the old man that grows corrupt according to deceitful lusts. When it comes to the desires of our flesh, we are supposed to put them off, *not* put them on. We are supposed to starve the old man, not continue to feed him.

Instead, today in the name of worship we are seeing behaviour that once was considered shameful or immoral being displayed *publicly* on a regular basis *in the church*. Let me give you some specific instances of what I mean.

Immodest dress

Am I the only one who has noticed that some of the ladies in the worship teams or performing special music are wearing provocative dresses or tight, revealing clothing, and doing so on the platform in full view of the congregation? They are imitating secular female artists who dress that way purposely to tease and tempt men.

Ladies, the apostle Paul commanded you to dress in 'modest apparel, with propriety and moderation' (1 Timothy 2:9-10). He also said we are not to have even the *slightest* hint of immorality in our lives (Ephesians 5:3). My wife Judy tells me that a woman's style of dress can do much more than just 'hint', it can advertise.

I admit that my old sinful nature retains certain lustful tendencies and I continually have to guard my eyes in order to starve such desires. I am not alone. So do millions of other Christian men and boys. Ladies, please do not put a stumbling block in front of us with your immodest apparel.

Sensual movement

Is it proper and modest for Christian ladies or gentlemen to dance and sway in a worldly manner, while they sing praise and worship songs to God? No. They are doing this because of the rock music style and beat, not because they want to dance before the Lord like David did.

When you combine the sensual dancing with the immodest dress of the women on the platform, you place a *very large* stumbling block in front of the men of the congregation.

The danger of misplaced passion

Passion is an important ingredient in worship and praise — but this same passion can become a snare to unwary participants. Does your worship team mix single or divorced men and women together with those who are married? That is an open door for sexual immorality. If you put hot-blooded males and females into a passionate rock music group, there will be strong temptation for sexual sins. CCM styles facilitate an atmosphere where a female's innate desire to have emotional intimacy with a man can easily be achieved. The problem is, most of the time that man is not her husband. This leads to something called emotional adultery, a problem that can later lead to physical adultery.

A cosy mix of men and women in a worship team can also be enough to cause a division between a spouse who is on the team, and one who is not. It invites jealousy and mistrust. Judy saw a unity between the men and women in my groups that did not exist between their spouses who were outside the group. This is a stumbling block to the spouse on the outside. Even if there is no actual *physical* sin between the members of the worship team, this type of atmosphere is still wrong because it can weaken the marriage bond, leading it to break down in the future. Sadly, this has happened in one of my former groups.

I'm sure there must be at least one Contemporary worship leader who is now thinking, 'Come on, Dan, you're being a Puritan! My people can handle this without sinning.' Be very careful, friend. As leaders of the church, we are never to lead the saints into temptation or any hint of immorality. Why would you even permit an environment of potential sexual temptation and emotional adultery to exist in your church service? Of course, this type of sin can rear its ugly head in any musical environment, but CCM creates an atmosphere that actually *fosters* it.

Extreme personal intimacy in public worship

We all desire intimacy in our relationship with the Lord. When we worship together, some of us like to see it displayed in others. This makes us feel good. We all want to reach a point of heightened praise and emotions that tells us, 'Yes! God is here!' So we use CCM to create this atmosphere. We dim the lights, we design the music to move people where we want to take them and we create the special mood, the right atmosphere.

What is wrong with this? It is *exactly* what the world does to create sexual intimacy. Secular musicians use the same music styles and environmental methods to draw people into sexual intimacy with them. It is all about bringing sensuality into the public forum and breaking down all of our sexual inhibitions.

Satan has used this approach for years to encourage people to commit sexual immorality. We cannot use these unholy methods to manipulate God into 'drawing near' to us or fooling ourselves into believing we are drawing closer to him. In fact, what we are really accomplishing is to give Satan more opportunities to ensnare and bring about the spiritual downfall of many unsuspecting victims.

A. W. Tozer was blunt in his assessment of this pseudo-intimacy:

> Much of the singing in certain types of meetings has in it more of romance than it has of the Holy Ghost. Both words and music are designed to rouse the libidinous [lewd; full of lust]. Christ is courted with a familiarity that reveals a total ignorance of Who He is. *It is not the reverent intimacy of the adoring saint but the impudent familiarity of the carnal lover* (emphasis added).[1]

When our worship style imitates the world so closely, we give Satan too good an opportunity to replace the truth with feelings. Just as the intimacy of a marriage relationship should be kept private, I also believe that demonstrating deep spiritual intimacy with the Lord is best kept private.

CCM's baggage

CCM is stuck with this stigma of immorality, because the music styles carry with them the baggage of the world's immorality. It does not matter if you change the lyrics. It does not matter if you change the musicians. It does not matter if you change the record labels. It does not matter if you ask God to sanctify it. Rock music and all its children, and by association CCM, can and will corrupt the morals of everyone who practises it.

CCM proponents should stop trying to defend their actions and accept what the rest of the world already knows: rock music produces an atmosphere that has no place in the church! Let's not continue to give Satan a foothold in our worship services to seduce the saints. It is time for *all* of us to accept this reality, to repent of our actions, and to stop allowing any hint of immorality or opportunity for sexual temptation into the worship service. We need to remember that we are worshipping the almighty God, the Holy One of Israel, and his Son Jesus Christ, who now sits at the right hand of the Father in the throne room of heaven.

7.
Splitting churches

In a church that makes the change from traditional to contemporary music, there is usually a group of Traditionals who are offended by it. What happens to them when they try to express their concerns? What sort of treatment do they receive from the Contemporaries? Such a change ends too often in a church split, with the Traditionals blamed for their divisive or judgemental attitude. But through a closer look at how Contemporary leaders treat Traditionals who dare to discern, we will learn who is really to blame for splitting churches.

As stated earlier, some Contemporaries regard those who disagree or try to stand in their way as 'poor, tradition-bound people who just do not understand the heart of worship' and who are 'standing in the way of what God wants to do'. This divisive spirit has infected many worship leaders today as it did me. The leaders actually believe that God is trying to do something special through the use of their own preferred music style. They attend P&W seminars and catch a vision for change. They rush back to the church, eager to implement the latest P&W trend in the next service! Anyone who stands in their way will be neutralized with the label of 'legalistic Pharisee', or will be put on the defensive with some of the arguments outlined in this book.

It seems to be the case now that anyone who criticizes anything is wrong and mean-spirited. And more and more often, when it comes to a choice between losing long-time members of our church or our pet music programmes, Contemporaries decide that *people* are also expendable.

It is no wonder long-time members feel that they must leave the church, sometimes one that they may have helped to start or build. They are made to feel as if *they* did something wrong, when in reality it is the Contemporaries who are causing the problem with their offensive music choices, their insensitivity and their often arrogant attitude. Because of this, I lay the blame of splitting churches over music at the feet of Contemporary leaders who insist on the adoption of their music agenda without regard to the conscience and discernment of others. Only recently have I become aware of the great pain this can cause, when my own family left a church over a disagreement in music philosophy. I believe God wanted me to experience the hurt, so I could finally wake up to what I was doing to others.

Sadly, I have also heard pastors make insensitive and divisive statements, such as 'If they don't like it, there are other churches in town for them to attend'; or 'This is only a matter of style and preference, it's not worth fighting over.' (In all fairness, this same divisive attitude is not limited solely to pastors caught up in the CCM movement.)

Pastor Warren openly admits that a church will inevitably lose members over music changes:

> Once you have decided on the style of music you're going to use in worship, you have set the direction of your church in far more ways than you realize. It will determine the kind of people you attract, the kind of people you keep, and *the kind of people you lose* (emphasis added).[1]

When a pastor accepts the CCM movement, the members of his flock who, like Judy, discern a problem coming into the church, no longer have a shepherd to protect them. Instead they have a shepherd who has decided that some sheep are worth losing. But when is a pastor allowed to drive away sheep from his flock? We can all agree that a pastor has the biblical imperative to send away a divisive 'sheep' after scriptural church discipline has failed to bring about repentance; but does the Bible also teach that a pastor may drive away the good and faithful sheep because of a new *music programme*? Of course not, but Contemporary pastors have found justification for it, nonetheless.

Many Traditionals have felt the church door hit them on the way out. They have been forced out of the protection of the fold by a pastor enamoured with the power of CCM; and then left to a dangerous journey through wolf-infested wilderness to find a shepherd who will not put controversial music styles above the needs of his flock. Then, to add insult to injury, after being told that they were selfish and did not care about the unchurched who are going to hell because of the Traditionals' music preference, and after some have left the church they love, the purpose-driven church abandons all pretence that 'CCM is for our evangelistic seeker services.' Sooner or later, *all the services* are devoted to CCM styles. That is the real agenda.

Take a moment to ponder what you have just read. This is a grievous sin, pastors. You have no biblical imperative to push Christians out of the door in order to smooth the way for CCM or any other new fad or style. If you are a pastor who has allowed this to happen, it is not too late to repent and put it right.

I realize now that I too hurt people and caused divisions when I promoted CCM and argued with Traditionals. I led transitions from traditional to contemporary, and doubtless there were people who left their churches as a direct result. Through my arrogance, I caused hurtful divisions within my own family. I have confessed this sin to the Lord, repented of it, and now I ask their forgiveness.

Have you been hurt like this? Do you bear the scars of a church-music fight? Have you left a church under these circumstances? I can assure you that God will heal your hurt and place you in a safe fellowship, if you can let go of any bitterness held in your heart.

If you are in a church that is struggling over this, please give your pastor a copy of this book[2] and ask him to consider the spiritual consequences of CCM in the church.

8.
Isn't this just a matter of personal preference and taste?

At age seventeen, my son Chris came to me in tears and frustration over a musical incident in the youth group. The youth pastor had invited a Christian rock band to lead a worship concert during the weekly youth meeting. He had a sincere motive: they could invite their unsaved friends from school, who could then be reached through the music. Chris characterized this as making church music sound 'cool' and non-offensive to secular friends. The band played hard rock, with extremely loud volume and a driving beat that literally made Chris shake, and feel as if it had taken over his heartbeat.

As the band played on, Chris could not stay in the room. The music had a bad affect on his spirit, and he stepped out into the hallway to escape from its influence. The youth pastor followed and confronted Chris, telling him that as a peer leader in the group he was expected to support this concert. The pastor asked him to go back inside. Chris tried to explain his apprehension and his confused spirit, but he was unable to express adequately the sense of oppression he felt. The pastor, a man deeply involved in the CCM movement and well versed in the arguments in favour of it, led Chris to feel guilty, as if there was something wrong with his attitude towards the concert. This spiritual leader, who Chris admired and loved, was challenging my son with his own persuasive opinion.

The youth pastor and I were good friends and partners in the music ministry. He sang on the worship team and we often prayed together. But I needed to confront him. We had a gracious conversation about the incident, and he used some of the CCM arguments that are covered in this book. He challenged me with his belief that, when it comes to music and other questionable areas of Christian living, God accepts different personal preferences and tastes in the church. He said we are not to judge one another in these areas because it is a matter of individual taste. He also believed God is a god of diversity and creativity — after all, he made all different kinds of people and gave them different tastes in music.

This is a very powerful and persuasive argument for accepting CCM in church. I told him that I could not accept that argument at face value — I needed chapter and verse in the Bible. So I spent a considerable time studying what the Bible has to say about questions of personal preference and taste.

As a result of my Bible study, I am convinced that God really *does* care about our tastes and preferences because we live on this earth as his representatives. I found clear principles in Scripture that both teach us to avoid diligently any personal preference or style that could be associated with evil, and also confirm there are limits to our freedom to use our personal preferences. In many churches today, Contemporaries are using music styles that violate both these biblical principles.

From the Scriptures, I learned that in order to live a holy life that is pleasing to God, I must be cautious about the styles or fashions I embrace. And I must put my brother's needs above my own. Music happens to be an especially important issue for me, but I also learned that I need to make careful choices about what I watch on television, what I read, where I surf on the Web and where I travel on vacation.

I would now like to point you to some of the principles I learned from my study. I am not going to be dogmatic about my interpretation of the related verses. If you are born again, the Holy Spirit is your teacher and I am confident that sooner or later you will be led to the same general conclusions. And like the apostle Paul, I too will not force anyone to follow men's rules. But I have no qualms at all about trying to persuade you of the best way to handle a dispute over music styles.

1. Avoid *any* preference or style that can be associated with evil

'Abstain from every form of evil' (1 Thessalonians 5:22).

Many Christians today would rather not discuss 1 Thessalonians 5:22 because its application would require them to give up some of their cherished worldly practices. But its benefits are there for all to see. Paul addresses not just the acts of evil themselves but also the very *form* of evil. The Greek word translated as 'form' also carries the idea of a view, an appearance, a fashion, or a shape. The Bible calls for abstinence. That means we should avoid it, or restrain ourselves from indulging in it.

In 1 Peter 2:11, the apostle Peter warns us to avoid fleshly lusts, desires that are forbidden to us, that come out of our sinful nature. I believe our desires to have CCM styles in the church come directly from this sinful nature. Peter adds another sobering reason for abstinence: these desires war against our souls. Carnal, fleshly desires literally conduct a military campaign against the right principles and moral precepts of God. This is not a physical war; this is spiritual warfare.

Not only are we to avoid evil and fleshly lusts (and even the appearance of such), we should not even have a *hint* of immorality among us. Ephesians 5:3 states: 'But fornication and all uncleanness or covetousness, let it not even be named among you, as is fitting for saints.' The New International Version renders this verse: 'But among you there must not be even a hint of sexual immorality, or of any kind of impurity, or of greed, because these are improper for God's holy people.'

Jesus took this whole idea further when he said, 'But I say to you that whoever looks at a woman to lust for her has already committed adultery with her in his heart' (Matthew 5:28). By this statement, he equated the evil and lust we contemplate in our unseen thought life with the evil and lust that can be seen by everyone. Therefore, not only must we avoid evil and lust themselves, and avoid any hint or the appearances of them, we must also avoid those things that would encourage us to even *consider* any such sin in our minds.

Let us apply this to the practice of using CCM in worship services. When we bring rock music styles into the church, we violate this principle of abstinence from the appearance of evil. We are guilty of:

- Embracing a form (or a carrier) of evil, because CCM imitates the same worldly music and performance styles that are used alongside all kinds of immorality.
- Indulging our fleshly lusts and polluting our thought life.
- Committing treason against the Lord by aiding and abetting the enemy in the war against God's principles and precepts.

Application

We should avoid all music styles that could be associated in any way with today's evil and immorality. We should not use them in church or in our private lives.

2. My freedom in Christ has limits

'All things are lawful for me, but not all things are helpful; all things are lawful for me, but not all things edify' (1 Corinthians 10:23).

The Greek word translated as 'helpful' literally means 'to bear together; to contribute an advantage to; to be better or good for; to be profitable'. This is our first lesson on our limits to freedom in Christ: everything we do should be good for both others and ourselves. If anything is not going to benefit all concerned, even though it is permissible for me, I should choose not to do it.

In this chapter, Paul is bringing a warning for us from Israel's history. Verse 6 says, 'Now these things became our examples, to the intent that we should not lust after evil things as they also lusted.' Paul is warning us about the dangers of idol worship. In verse 14, he progresses into a discussion over eating meat sacrificed to idols, with the plea for the Corinthian believers to 'flee from idolatry'. To 'flee' literally means 'to run away or to escape from' idolatry. Paul obviously did not want us to associate either with idols or with those who practise idol worship. The Greek word for idolatry, eidololatreia, means 'image worship'. That definition could easily apply to the way some Christian teens and adults treat CCM artists.

Eating meat which has been sacrificed to idols was a contemporary controversy in the early church. Some brothers ate it without any problem, while others were very offended by it. Paul takes us through some very sensitive ground here, showing us the wide latitude of grace concerning behaviour that touched on pagan practices. He allows the eating of this meat as long as the brother doing so is not pricked in his own conscience. But if a brother is present who is offended by it, then it is better to stop.

Paul does not *command* the first brother to stop eating the meat, without any further discussion. In fact, Paul says in verse 29: 'For why is my liberty judged by another man's conscience?' But in verses 32 and 33 he quickly goes on to say that the *right* choice in this matter is to 'Give no offence, either to the Jews or to the Greeks or to the church of God, just as I also please all men in all things, not seeking my own profit, but the profit of many, that they may be saved.'

I see a clear principle here that places boundaries around our selfish, worldly preferences, calling us to a much higher good. We should sacrifice our freedom willingly for the sake of our brother.

Application

When it comes to our music preferences for public worship, we should honour our brother's needs above our own freedom in Christ.

3. Don't let your preferences put obstacles in your brother's path

'But beware lest somehow this liberty of yours become a stumbling block to those who are weak' (1 Corinthians 8:9).

'But when you thus sin against the brethren, and wound their weak conscience, you sin against Christ' (1 Corinthians 8:12).

Again, the context here is the controversy over some church members who were eating meat known publicly to have been from animals that were sacrificed to pagan idols. I believe there is a principle here that goes beyond just meat, one that we can apply to *any* practice where there is disagreement in the church.

In chapter 8, Paul says a brother has the liberty to eat this meat if it does not trouble his conscience. Liberty means the power of doing or not doing; free choice; freedom. But again, as we saw earlier, his freedom is not unlimited: it has boundaries. Back in Romans chapter 14, we are told not to judge each other's preferences when it comes to eating meat or observing certain sacred days. Romans 14:13 begins: 'Therefore let us not judge one another anymore.' This is a favourite biblical quote for the Contemporaries. But what about the *rest* of that verse? 'But rather resolve this, not to put a stumbling block or a cause to fall in our brother's way.' A stumbling block in Greece was figuratively a stone of stumbling, meaning a cause for falling, an occasion of sinning, an offence.

Once again Paul is very clear that the stronger brother is to be considerate of the weaker one. The Greek phrase for 'those who are weak' refers to those whose minds are easily disturbed, who have a weakness of the mind, where there is doubt, vacillation or hesitation about a particular matter. The weaker brother is easily disturbed by the action of the stronger brother. He is especially susceptible to the stumbling block placed there by the stronger brother.

What about the so-called 'stronger' brother? Is he stronger in all matters of the faith, and is he more mature than the weaker brother? I believe Paul means this brother is stronger *only* in this particular matter. We need to be careful not to equate this particular strength of conscience with overall maturity in Christ. I would argue that a mature Christian is one who is closer to conformity with Christ, and it therefore follows that this person would be *less* involved with questionable worldly practices like this. Too often we tend to consider contemporary praise and worship leaders as stronger and more mature than the 'weak' Traditional. I believe we have that completely the wrong way round!

In 1 Corinthians 8:13 Paul concludes: 'Therefore, if food makes my brother stumble, I will never again eat meat, lest I make my brother stumble.' Paul is pledging that he will abstain from practices he knows will offend his brothers. Romans 14:21 puts it this way: 'It is good neither to eat meat nor drink wine *nor do anything* by which your brother stumbles or is offended or is made weak' (emphasis added).

Application

If the music we prefer is an offence to our weaker brother and causes him to stumble, we should never listen to that music in front of him again.

4. Be a builder, *not* part of a demolition crew

*'Therefore let us pursue the things which make for peace and the things by which one may edify another' (Romans 14:19).*To edify literally means to be a house builder; to confirm; to build up.

In Romans 14, Paul is discussing how to handle disputes caused by personal preferences for worldly things. In the Roman church, there were disputes over food and holidays. Paul does not seem to take sides; instead his argument levels the playing field between the two opposing positions and does not give either of them any cause for pride. He reminds us that all Christians are accountable to God. In verse 17, he states that the kingdom of God is not a matter of eating and drinking but of 'righteousness and peace and joy in the Holy Spirit'. As a result, then, we should make every effort to act in a way that leads to peace, not conflict. We should find ways to build each other up in the faith, not tear each other down.

Verse 20 states: 'Do not destroy the work of God for the sake of food.' To destroy literally means 'to demolish'. Demolition crews build nothing; they only tear buildings down.

Application

We should be builders in the body of Christ, not destroyers.

Conclusion

The argument that 'It is only a matter of personal preference and taste' is a crucial justification for CCM use in church and therefore it must be refuted. Whenever a Contemporary uses this argument, do not be afraid to confront him or her if the music style is offensive to you. We must also practise what we preach and apply the above principles consistently to other matters in the church. Hypocritical Traditionals are exactly what the Contemporary needs to win others to his or her cause.

We need churches that are full of Christians who practise the principles of edification, who sacrifice their personal freedoms, who give preference to the needs of others and who avoid diligently all forms of evil. Then, instead of engaging in the current conflict over music, we would be trying to outdo each other to please and edify. Music ministers would care more about their congregation than the performance and style. Never again would anyone have to leave our church over music. Could we ever agree on a music style that is non-offensive to everyone? I believe the evidence is clear that yes, we could agree on several styles of music that are non-controversial and far enough removed from any contemporary associations with immorality. That is how our churches operated before the 1970s.

9.
Isn't music amoral?

A well-known Christian songwriter gave a lecture last year at a leading Christian college in Ohio. He played single notes on the piano and asked his student audience if those notes were good or evil. He then played the theme from *Mr Rogers' Neighborhood* (a popular television series for toddlers) and the tune 'Moon River', and asked if this music was Christian or non-Christian. From these simple examples he concluded, much to the delight of most of the students, that music itself is amoral. The belief that all music is amoral is a very popular argument and foundational to the contemporary music philosophy.

This perspective was actually institutionalized at one time into a confession known as the 'Christian Rocker's Creed': 'We hold these truths to be self-evident, that all music was created equal — that no instrument or style of music is in itself evil — that the diversity of musical expression which flows forth from man is but one evidence of the boundless creativity of our Heavenly Father.'[1]

Paradoxically, this is also one of the weakest arguments for the justification of using any music style for praise and worship. There is quite simply no support in the Bible for this viewpoint; unless, that is, you believe that if the Bible says nothing specific about music's morality, then it *must* be amoral. Do not use that reasoning — it can lead to error about all the other grey areas not specifically discussed in the Bible. There does not seem to be any historical precedent for this view either. Claims of music's moral neutrality seem to have surfaced at the same time as the rise of CCM in the 1980s.

Despite the dubious support for this argument, many Christians truly *believe* this statement as if it were the absolute truth. Perhaps they just want simple answers to complex questions and conflicts. I've heard it repeated again and again as if it had some real and authoritative weight. Anyone who accepts this claim is presumably free from any restraints or any questions about the appropriateness of their music choices. If they simply declare, without biblical proof of any kind, that all music is amoral and only the lyrics matter, then no Traditional can ever again judge their music. Pastor Warren shows how this is done:

> I reject the idea that music styles can be judged as either 'good' or 'bad' music. Who decides this? The kind of music you like is determined by your background and culture.
>
> Music is nothing more than an arrangement of notes and rhythms; it's the words that make a song spiritual. There is no such thing as 'Christian music', only Christian lyrics. If I were to play a tune for you without any words, you wouldn't know if it was a Christian song or not.[2]

As a result of accepting this argument, Contemporaries do not see the need for any discussion about music styles. Once a person goes along with the 'music is amoral' argument, to him or her the debate is over before it begins. He will usually change the subject from the music to the lyrics, and waste a lot of time discussing the obvious point that lyrical content must conform to biblical truth.

What exactly does *amoral* mean? From *Webster's New World College Dictionary*, amoral means 'not to be judged by criteria of morality; neither moral or immoral; without moral sense or principles, incapable of distinguishing between right and wrong'.

What is morality? It is moral quality or character, rightness or wrongness; in accord with the principles or standards of right conduct.

The argument implies that music should not be judged as being moral or immoral, because music has no moral sense, and is incapable of being either right or wrong. In other words, music is neutral. I agree that the generic *concept* of music is neutral. Notes and chords by themselves are benign. God created melody, harmony and rhythm and as concepts they are not offensive in any way; in fact they are pleasing by design.

But unlike the overly simple example used by the songwriter, we are dealing with something far more complex. When Contemporaries say music is amoral, they are not really speaking of generic notes, chords, melody, harmony and rhythms. They are defending a specific musical style that is represented by a particular song they like. No one in a contemporary (or traditional) service is singing just the generic music notes and chords. Everyone is singing someone's song. Since humans write it, the song cannot help but inherit a certain style from the human creator. Do you believe that man can corrupt music? I'm sure you would have to agree that he can.

Do you now see the falsehood in the argument that music is amoral and neutral? Yet, many are deceived into believing the big lie that *all* music styles are acceptable for use in worship and praise. No one actually plays or sings generic and neutral music in a service. The songs are written with a specific style. For this reason alone, I say the 'music is amoral' argument is irrelevant. The real issue we must address then is whether or not a music *style* can be associated with a moral dimension. The answer is 'yes' and that is very easy to prove.

Is the rock music style used in so much CCM associated with any particular moral dimension? I argue that it is clearly and unequivocally associated with immorality, especially promiscuous and adulterous sex, glorification of drugs, and rebellion against authority. But, Dan, you must mean the secular godless lyrics, not the music. No, I mean the music style itself. Decades of rock music in our culture have permanently stamped that music style with the dimension of immorality. Changing the lyrics and substituting Christian musicians cannot remove that stigma.

That is the very reason why so many Christians are offended when rock music or a close musical relative are used inside the church. They are rightfully offended because the music style reminds them of its immoral dimension. They quickly associate the music with sensuality, depravity and rebellion. The music is 'guilty by association'. I have heard some CCM apologists complain that it is unfair to judge rock music that way; that it should be deemed innocent until proven guilty. I do not agree that secular laws apply equally to church music. That must answer to God's higher law.

Why do you think Contemporaries have such a problem when Christians who are rightly offended by the use of this music style in church dare to speak up? The reason is obvious. In order for their controversial music styles to be accepted into the church, Contemporaries had to exchange the truth for the deceptive argument that music is amoral. Now they must defend that belief against any challenge; if this defence fails, they will be forced (as I was) to accept the unacceptable: that some of their music styles belong to evil, not to good.

Some early Contemporary must have conjured up this argument in defence of the rock music style. When something this absurd is repeated enough times over the years, it can start to sound reasonable. That is why, again, we must rebuke such a false argument. Music concepts may be amoral or neutral, but all music *styles* have a moral dimension because they are so easily and unavoidably associated with some worldly attachment. The question we should now ask is this: With what moral dimension is *my* favourite music associated?

10.
But God made music — isn't all music inherently good?

Directly related to the 'music is amoral' argument is the other common half-truth used to justify the use of CCM in the church: that all music is inherently good. I believe Contemporaries have misinterpreted a biblical principle to come up with this argument. True, God made all *created* things and called them good. Man is his creation. Sound is his creation. The concepts of melody, harmony and rhythm are his creation. He created order. But does God write the song that contains his sound with his melody, harmony and order? Of course not. Man writes the song.

Contemporaries are trying to justify the use of a specific music style that is represented in the real world by actual songs. Their argument is that God made 'music'. But what is this generic, universal music that God made? It is like Lego, a popular children's activity. Lego consists of individual building blocks that by themselves have little value. Assembling them into a final work, such as a truck or a fire station, gives them a recognizable value from which we can evaluate the child's creativity. It is the same with the concept of generic music. God created the generic notes and gave us the concepts of beauty and order for the sounds. They are the building blocks.

Here I would like to repeat and emphasize what we discussed in an earlier chapter. No one in a CCM service is singing this generic music. They are singing someone's song that *contains* music. Since humans build it, the song cannot help but inherit a certain style from the human creator. Man can corrupt God's creation.

The biblical record

Additionally, I do not trust the argument that all music is or can be good, because of the biblical record. The first musical reference in the entire Bible is not in Psalms or Chronicles, as many believe. It is not in the stories of David or the song of Moses. The first mention of music is found very early in Genesis 4:21, where we are introduced to Jubal, the father of all musicians: 'He was the father of all those who play the harp and flute.' Our modern band and orchestra instruments can probably be traced to the handiwork of Jubal and his descendants.

Furthermore, the first musician named in the Bible was a direct descendant of Cain, whom God had judged so severely because he used his own *personal preferences* in worship! Ponder that for a moment. God told Cain that his personal style of worship was unacceptable because it violated the specific rules given by God. Cain was infuriated by this rejection and extremely jealous that God accepted his brother Abel's worship. Cain murdered Abel and was banished from the presence of the Lord and his family.

Cain's descendants continued to disobey God. They were so wicked that when they intermarried with the line of Seth, God decided to destroy them with the Flood. This was the heritage and environment of Jubal. Because of the corruption inherent in man's musical creations, Christian musicians need to be very, very careful with their musical talents and music choices, which are so easily corrupted by our sinful nature and desires.

The first musicians specifically set apart for God's praise seem to appear much later in 1 Chronicles 16, when David assigned the first official worship leaders in Israel to minister before the Ark of the Covenant. It is important to note that David chose Levites, who were sanctified or set apart to God's service. Leading worship to God in the Old Testament was not something allowed for just any musician, nor would they use just any music. Everything and everyone was carefully set apart, out of reverence and fear of the awesome Jehovah. Even though we are not under the law today, we find an important principle here for selecting the musicians and the music for use in a worship service.

The Contemporary may respond with: 'Why surely God can redeem the "bad" music and use it for his glory.' I challenge him or her to show me the chapter and verse where God does this. Otherwise, that is just a personal opinion and I will not stake the integrity of my music ministry on it.

11.
Show me where the Bible says that rock music is evil

This challenge is currently circulating around those Christian college campuses where you can hear any style of music claimed in the name of Jesus, regardless of its worldly associations. We can add this to the 'Show me where' hall of fame. Those classic comments made by sceptics and carnal Christians throughout the ages.

Here are some of the other classic 'show me' arguments:

- Show me where the Bible says it is wrong to have a few beers.
- Show me where the Bible says I should not smoke.
- Show me where the Bible says I should not get high on marijuana.
- Show me where the Bible says it is wrong to spend holidays in Las Vegas.
- Show me where the Bible says I should not play the lottery.
- And that current favourite among the Contemporaries: show me where the Bible says that we should only use hymns in church.

I am using sarcasm here to make a point. Sometimes when we are confronted with a controversial grey area that is not clearly condemned in the Bible, we respond with this 'show me' defence. The truth is, the Bible does not specifically mention rock music or any other contemporary music style. Nor for that matter does the Bible clearly condemn the other behaviours and choices listed above. That is why this clever little challenge wins many arguments by quickly silencing the person who opposes CCM use.

Most Traditionals are looking for a quick, devastating soundbite to defeat this challenge. Although the answer is much more complex, I have some suggestions. When someone says, 'Show me where the Bible says that rock music is evil', you could reply: 'Show me where the Bible says that...':

- '...God is pleased you chose the same music style as Madonna, Hootie and the Blowfish, and the Dave Matthews Band.'
- '...you should vigorously defend the favourite music style of this world.'
- '...it's OK to use the same music style as the sex and drug culture.'
- '...God waived that "abstain from all appearance of evil" clause just for you.'

One of these stinging responses may actually work; but if the Contemporary is well practised in this game you can then expect a direct attack on your music style preferences. For example, if you prefer classical music styles in church, the Contemporary may retort: 'Your classical music is just as secular and worldly as my rock music!'

This sort of debating style reminds me of the time early in my Christian life when I told another believer that people who ate high-fat foods were just as sinful as those who smoked. This was prompted because he was criticizing the smokers (among whose ranks I used to belong). That's futile logic — of course, both must ensure they take care of their bodies. But when we argue over the grey areas in the Bible, we tend to try and drag everyone else down into the mire along with us. This is how we defend the indefensible.

If you are confronted with that sort of reply, ask the person to prove that your classical music has the same stigma of immorality as rock music. The burden is on them to explain logically how that music style causes offence in today's church. In fact, classical music today is so far removed from any of the supposed immorality of the original composers and performers, that no one can honestly claim it is generally and closely associated with evil.

Can classical music still be used by Satan? It's certainly conceivable, although it is rarely heard of those days. Composers such as Mozart and Beethoven are said to have lived less than perfect lives yet they left us with music that is almost universally considered as beautiful. Some operas do have suggestive librettos that hint at adultery, fornication and disobedience to authority. But I personally would not use any opera in church. Yet if I ever meet a believer who is truly offended by the use of classical music styles for praise and worship, I will be compelled to practise the biblical principles on preference and taste covered earlier.

Can rock music be used by Satan? What a question! The very names of many of the performing groups — Black Sabbath, KISS (Knights in Satan's Service), AC/DC, Sex Pistols, to name but a few — advertise the profane associations. Rock music is obviously connected with certain evil things and people. The Bible commands us to avoid and abstain from the appearance of evil. Put two and two together and you get four.

I do not really believe that any clever and quick response will actually change the mind of the person with a 'show me where' attitude. As with any other controversial grey area in our Christian walk, we must be diligent to learn the principles of Scripture that apply to our personal choices and behaviour. I offered some of these principles in the chapter on personal preference and taste.

Yet there is so much more involved in learning how to live a life set apart to Christ. 'Be holy' is a command to God's people that is found throughout the Scriptures. Personal holiness is demanded by Christ, the Apostles and the entire Old Testament. Holiness means to be set apart *for* God *from* the world. But reality is tough, and the highway to holiness is very narrow as it winds through our culture of sensuality and materialism. Yet Christians are called to walk that straight and narrow road, a walk that requires us to avoid anything that hints of immorality. That means we sometimes have to shun things like rock music. Will we fall into sin on the way? Yes. But we should never use that as an excuse to bring the appearance of evil into the church with our music.

12.
Doesn't the Bible teach we can use all things to reach people?

This argument is used to justify any contemporary music style in the church as long as it is used to reach the lost. As a contemporary worship leader, I used it often. The argument contends that CCM can reach the lost better than traditional church music, because that is what the lost are used to hearing and they will be more receptive to the gospel when they hear it presented with their style of music. Therefore, it follows that we can use any style of music as long as the goal is salvation. Let's examine the supporting verse, 1 Corinthians 9:22: 'to the weak I became as weak, that I might win the weak. *I have become all things to all men,* that I might by all means save some.'

The phrase in italics is used to justify CCM as a means to the end of salvation. When the deception includes a Bible verse to back it up, it becomes extremely powerful within the church. Too many Christians do not know how to study their Bibles and can easily be persuaded by verses taken out of context or interpreted in error. Even pastors who otherwise have very strong Bible study and interpretation skills seem to be falling for this deception. This is evident from the speed with which so many pastors have enthusiastically accepted CCM into their church services, and how few of them are taking a stand against it. That is a major reason why I believe the CCM deceptions have caught on so easily with so little resistance. Pastors are to guard the sheep from deception, not open the gate and let it in.

This is another attempt to use a righteous motive as a cover-up for a controversial musical preference. From a superficial reading of the passage Paul seems to be saying that he tried to blend in with those whom he hoped to convert as a means of drawing them to salvation. But in context, this verse has nothing at all to do with music styles — it is part of a discussion about Paul's servant attitude towards evangelism. In this passage Paul is also defending his ministry, among both the Jews and the Gentiles, and describing his attitude towards observance of the Old Testament law. He cites three groups: those under the law — the Jews; those without law — the Gentiles; and the weak — those Christians who are not sure whether or not the law applies to them and so they lack confidence. But even here Paul assures the reader that he considers himself 'not being without law toward God, but under law toward Christ' (9:21). In other words, he respected the scruples of all groups, and *where no principle was trampled on*, conformed his behaviour to theirs for their benefit. To take verse 22 out of this context in an attempt to justify questionable (at best) worship practices or evangelistic methods is indefensible.

Based on the overwhelming weight of Paul's writing in the New Testament, how can anyone infer that he would use, or approve the use of, such controversial means as rock music? Using Paul's statement here to defend CCM in the church is unbiblical and it is also very unfair to the Apostle, implying that he would actually approve of using *any* carnal or worldly means to salvation.

This is the same Paul who was so concerned about holy living, and admonished us to put to death the deeds of the body (Romans 8:13) and to flee from youthful lusts (2 Timothy 2:22). This is also the same Paul who taught us to honour a brother's needs and weaknesses over our own. (See also chapter 8.)

We should not accept just any worldly method to reach the lost. Instead we must discern carefully what methods are acceptable for use in the kingdom of God.

13.
Should praise music be treated differently?

Judy and I have dear friends in Ohio who attend a church with a heritage of traditional music in the services. Recently, some of the members began a campaign to introduce contemporary music. (Ironically, this is a church to which several families fled to escape the contemporary changes I had implemented at another church nearby!) Our friends keep me informed of the debate, and I have shared much of this book with them to help them respond to the Contemporaries. This couple has been a great help and inspiration to me.

They brought to my attention an interesting twist to the issue I raised about the definition of worship. The Contemporary leaders at their church made a distinction between music styles that are appropriate for praise but not necessarily for worship. Though they might agree with Traditionals on the need to be careful with 'worship' music, they said that praise is separate and different and this allows room for upbeat contemporary music styles.

Psalm 150, the great and culminating praise psalm, is often used to support this view of praise music. Verses 4 and 5 in particular are used widely to justify the acceptance of CCM and dancing in our services. 'Praise Him with the timbrel and dance…; praise Him with loud cymbals; praise Him with clashing cymbals!'

I do not agree with that interpretation because it conveniently ignores the cultural and historical context of the Psalms in order to support CCM. Today we do not use the Hebrew instruments and worship styles to which these verses refer. We do not conform our services to the strict guidelines for reverence, purity and sanctification laid down by David in 1 Chronicles 16, guidelines which probably applied to the public use of this psalm. The Hebrews used percussion instruments, but I think it is ridiculous to, as some do, directly relate the drum set used by groups such as the Rolling Stones to the timbrel and cymbal mentioned in Psalm 150.

But I will go one step further than the Contemporaries who try to separate praise music from worship music. I now believe music in church is appropriate only to accompany the praise of God; we should *not* confuse music with worship. As I discussed earlier, biblical worship is the antithesis of the behaviour and attitudes we commonly exhibit during our modern music service. Praise is a much more biblical description of what we do: giving glory to God and Christ through songs, raising our hands in celebration, sharing testimonies of God's work in our lives, or quoting the Scriptures aloud to God. We are actually conducting 'praise', not worship, services. Therefore it is even more important to discuss what music styles are appropriate for praise.

Let's look closer at the specific meaning of 'praise'. What does the Bible mean by it? *Webster's New World College Dictionary* defines the verb 'to praise' as 'to commend the worth of; express approval and admiration of; to laud the glory of (God etc.) as in song; glorify, extol'. Praise implies an expression of approval, esteem or commendation. Our English word is derived from the Latin *pretium*, meaning worth or price. When we praise something, we express its worth. Compare this to the meaning of 'worship', which means to give honour and reverence to God. The only significant distinction in meaning is that *praise* implies an *audible expression* of approval and admiration, whereas *worship* describes rather an *attitude* of reverence and devotion. Praise and worship are like two peas, different but in the same pod.

In the Psalms, the Hebrew word translated praise is *halal* (the first part of hallelujah). *Strong's Concordance* defines *halal* as 'to be clear (originally of sound, but usually of colour); to shine'. It then goes on to describe meanings which evolved from the root such as 'to make a show, to boast; and thus to be (clamorously) foolish; to rave; to celebrate; (sing, be worthy of) praise, rage'. Some Contemporaries use the 'clamorously foolish' option to justify their extreme physical reactions and emotional outbursts during worship, but I cannot find a biblical context to support that.

As is the case with most Hebrew words, *halal* is incredibly rich in meaning. The first part of the definition seems the most apt: to be clear in sound or colour; to shine. When we *halal Jehovah*, do we shine for him? We should not praise him while we are tarnished or smudged by sin. Are the sounds and words of our praise clear to those who hear? We should not confuse them with music or lyrics that are muddled or distracting.

The New Testament translates several Greek words as praise.

- *Epainos* — laudation; approval; commendation; a commendable thing.
- *Ainos* — a story. Praise returned to God for benefits expected or received.
- *Aineo* — to sing praises, only of God.
- *Ainesis* — the act of praise, i.e. a thank offering.
- *Doxa* — glory; dignity, honour, praise, worship. Spoken of honour due or rendered.
- *Humneo* — to hymn, i.e. sing a religious ode; by implication, to celebrate (God) in song: sing a hymn of praise unto.[1]

Each Greek word brings its own rich and vibrant dimension of meaning to the praise of our Lord. *Epainos* is the most commonly used Greek word in the New Testament translated as praise. It has much in common with worship; both words convey the idea of giving honour to God.

What then is the relationship of praise to worship? As I stated in chapter 4, worship is the act and attitude of bowing down in reverence to God because of who he is, while praise is our expression of who God is. When we worship, we are in awe of God's greatness. When we praise, we speak of God's greatness. Can we praise God without worshipping? I don't believe so.

Can we worship God without praise? We need to remember that we can in fact worship God during a song of praise, in the midst of a prayer, when reading the Bible, listening to a sermon, looking at the mountains — indeed at any time when we realize the greatness of God, our own lowly estate in comparison, and we are driven undone to our knees (literally or figuratively in our hearts and minds). In this moment, there is often no joy, no uplifted spirit of praise. But after a genuine spiritual humbling, there is comfort from the Lord and he gives us a renewed heart to praise him (Psalm 51).

To return to the original question of this chapter, because praise is thought to be different from worship, does this allow room for praise songs that use CCM styles? I say no. God surely did not give praise music a special exemption from his standards of purity and virtue. We are not permitted to offend others just because we label it praise music instead of worship music. All music used in church should be selected using the same guidelines: it should not closely imitate worldly people and practices, and it should not be offensive to other Christians.

As we argue and bicker about music styles, perhaps we should take to heart what Matthew Henry said about Psalm 150:

The best music in God's ears is devout and pious affections, *non musica chordula, sed cor* — *not a melodious string, but a melodious heart.* Praise God with a strong faith; praise him with holy love and delight; praise him with an entire confidence in Christ; praise him with a believing triumph over the powers of darkness; praise him with an earnest desire towards him and a full satisfaction in him; praise him by a universal respect to all his commands; praise him by a cheerful submission to all his disposals; praise him by rejoicing in his love and solacing yourselves in his great goodness; praise him by promoting the interests of the kingdom of his grace; praise him by a lively hope and expectation of the kingdom of his glory[2] (emphasis added),

Hallelujah!

14.
Didn't Martin Luther and the Wesleys use contemporary music in church?

This is another common justification for CCM in the church. There is a myth about this that has grown out from an atom of truth, and Contemporaries love to repeat it as if it had the same weight as Scripture. The argument goes something like this: 'Well, you are being hypocritical by judging rock music, because *the church has always accepted contemporary music.*' As it was with me, I believe that 99.99% of Contemporaries have not personally researched church history to see if this is true, but have blindly accepted this as absolute truth from CCM leaders.

The CCM band Glad became popular promoters of this argument. At their concerts, they performed a musical skit around the notion that if Charles Wesley was alive at a different time in history, he would not have hesitated to use the popular music style of that day for his hymns. Glad produced a video of the skit, which was used to educate teens and recalcitrant adults that it was perfectly acceptable to use CCM in church. This is just one example of how this argument has been propagated throughout the ranks of Contemporaries.

It is time to take the teeth out of this deceptive little argument. An examination of church history will quickly demonstrate that this practice was the rare *exception* rather than the rule in church music. Furthermore, it will reveal that some Contemporaries have taken Luther and the Wesleys completely

out of their cultural and historical context to fabricate support
for their present positions.

It is said that Martin Luther and Charles Wesley set some of
their lyrics to popular folk tunes, including those sung in public
bars. Therefore, the argument goes, the church today should
be open and receptive to accept any contemporary music in
our services. After all, if it's good enough for Luther and Wesley,
it should be good enough for us today. But consider what
Makujina in his diligent historical research discovered about
Luther.

> Luther took the entire melody from only one secular song,
> 'I Came From an Alien Country' for 'From Heaven on
> High, I Come to You'. It first appeared in 1535 but four
> years later was replaced by an *original* tune from Luther,
> not the borrowed one. The secular tune does not reappear
> until after his death. The tune's use in worldly haunts would
> sully the sacred text and bring secular associations in-
> appropriate to worship, so Luther replaced it.[1]

Addressing the Wesley myth, Makujina went on to state:

> The example of the Wesleys does far more to undermine
> CCM's position than it does to buttress it. John [the brother
> of Charles who selected which of his brother's hymns were
> sung in church], who must be factored into the overall
> success of the Wesleyan hymnological revolution, was a
> far cry from the musical amoralists of today. As Darsey
> insists, 'Clearly Wesley was critically selective about the
> tunes he used for worship and he would not, contrary to
> today's popular notion, have considered raiding the bars
> indiscriminately for hymn tunes.'

I close with an urgent admonition from Darsey, who
expresses my sentiments exactly: 'No reasonable

interpretation of the facts can justify in the name of John
Wesley the freewheeling use of nearly any song that strikes
the fancy of modern worship.'[2]

Both Luther and Wesley were also said to have encountered strong resistance from the church of their day for introducing vulgar (i. e. common or popular) music into the worship
service. When they did, their music choices caused offence to
some in the congregation. But the Glad video poked fun at
those 'stuffy old saints'. It implied that Luther and Wesley were
just trying to reach the unchurched of their day but these Phari-
saical elements tried to stop them.

Now wait just a minute. Is there any basis in Scripture for
purposely offending the saints with music, even if you are a
great man of God such as Luther or Wesley? It is the brother
who causes the offence that should back off, not the one who is
offended. Luther certainly seems to have done so when he
substituted his own tune for the only secular tune he borrowed.
But the Contemporary's attitude implies exactly the opposite:
the *offended person* has sinned, not him! What insensitivity!
Christians were never called to offend each other. We do not
have the right to judge whether or not the offence felt by a
brother or sister in Christ is valid, before we agree to stop our
offending.

If you are a Contemporary, I have already anticipated your
next response. 'But what if *I* am offended by *traditional* music
styles? Shouldn't the Traditional offender stop using that style
too?' You need to give reasons why you are offended by traditional music. To this day, I have heard only two: it's boring or
it's irrelevant. But be honest. Does either of those reasons fall
into Paul's 'don't cause my brother to stumble and sin' cat-
egory? I do not think so. I have yet to hear legitimate reasons,
such as the fact that it has a sensual beat, is closely associated
with worldly lifestyles, or splits churches.

When challenged over his or her music choices, a Contemporary will often become defensive, saying to a Traditional, 'We are not to judge one another' when it comes to musical styles. Yet the *same* person will presume to judge whether or not your offence is valid! Or worse, the Contemporary will imply that all who resist are acting like Pharisees and justify his offensive music choice by pointing out that Jesus himself often offended the Pharisees.

This was too much for me to take. Who did we think we were — *Jesus*? Why was it so easy for Satan to trick us into seeing our Christian brethren (who otherwise live grace-filled lives before us) as Pharisees, just because they would not agree with us on music styles? Our brothers are *not* Pharisees and calling them such is a deep insult.

Another Contemporary comeback may ask why music that was so offensive in their day is acceptable to us today? Just as the drinking songs of past centuries have passed into acceptability after several generations, won't rock music also go through the same transition? Will it someday lose its immoral stigma? Even assuming the 'guilt by association' fades away, will it still produce the same sensual physical reactions? I don't think anyone can predict if and when that will happen. Remember the point I made in chapter 9, titled 'Isn't music amoral?' Music styles can and should be judged by their contemporary moral association. Wesley's and Luther's tunes, though controversial in their time, are no longer used in a controversial cultural context. On the other hand, the popular songs of today are controversial and should not be used in church.

A clever Contemporary may remind you that the organ was considered an evil instrument of the devil when it was first introduced to the church. Apparently some Christians strongly objected to its use in worship. Contemporaries look upon those Christians in the same way they treat Traditionals today. But do not be so quick to judge! We have the unfair advantage of looking back on them from a time and culture where the organ is very acceptable in church. Any objections of the past are long forgotten.

A Contemporary may also use the above example to justify the acceptance of contemporary instruments like the drum set or electric guitar. Have you ever encountered that argument? It alleges that if the organ was accepted in the church over time, then so will the drum set. The problem with this defence is obvious: *the Contemporary is simply not willing to* wait *100 years for the controversy to die down* — he wants his MTV *now*! No, what he really means is the drum set must be accepted *today*. I hope you now see both the foolishness and the arrogance of this defence.

But aren't there churches today that shun the use of organs or any musical instrument? I understand that there are. If ever I visit any, I will respect their preferences under the principle of 1 Corinthians 8. I will not look down on them, I will not gossip about them, and I will not try to change them.

When I look at a church, I am far more concerned about the way the Word of God is treated. If the Bible is misused to support its position on music, I will do my best to respond in love, not in contention; but I will speak up.

15.
Isn't CCM easier to sing
than traditional hymns?

As further justification for using CCM in the church service, some contemporary music ministers decided that the old hymns are just too hard for most people to sing. They argued that the words are too difficult to understand because of the old-fashioned English, that fewer churchgoers know how to sing four-part harmony, and that old church music will turn away visitors. One pastor stated the issue this way:

> The hymns contain an extremely rich heritage of worship music. Unfortunately, most people in the attraction group have had minimal exposure to the hymns. Those exposed to the hymns often have been exposed to hymns poorly done. This makes the use of hymns problematic.[1]

In contrast, CCM — almost always written with melody only — is believed to help everyone participate in worship and make visitors feel comfortable. This sounds like another good point.

So what is wrong with this argument? Well, it does not stand up in the real world. At the praise and worship services I led or participated in, I started to notice that everyone did *not* join in. In fact, some participants looked downright unhappy! I asked why and discovered two main reasons.

Difficult to learn

First of all, some people admitted they did not find it easy to learn the heavily syncopated melodies of CCM songs. Syncopation means beginning a musical tone on an *unaccented* beat and continuing it through the next accented beat, or beginning on the last half of a beat and continuing it through the first half of the following beat. It is common in many music styles, but some styles employ a heavy and continuous use of syncopation that produces the distinctive rock beat rhythm. You have heard this style of music many times: 'The Girl from Ipanema' is a classic older example. Every rock music song is heavily syncopated. It is fundamental to jazz and blues music too.

Heavily syncopated music is harder to learn, because it is difficult to sight read and it does not support our natural tendency to begin a note or phrase on the first half of the beat (or the 'down' beat). CCM, and all forms of rock music, overemphasizes the second half of the beat (or the 'back' beat). A skilled leader must teach others how to sing syncopated music, using constant repetition. In contrast, traditional and new conservative Christian music styles are easily taught because they tend to begin notes or phrases on the down beat.

It is also difficult to convey in writing the exact rhythm of a heavily syncopated composition. That is why if you've ever listened to a marching band that is playing an arrangement of a popular rock tune, you may have noticed that it never sounds quite the same as the original. The same is true when classically trained church musicians try to play CCM but cannot interpret it. You have to 'feel' this music to perform it.

Even white, suburbanite CCM rockers often struggle to correctly interpret blues or black gospel tunes because they lack the natural 'feel' for the music. Thomas Day described this dilemma in his reaction to the musical instructions given for a piece of contemporary music:

The tempo of the work is marked 'Walking Blues', in order to insure the right type of interpretation from the kind of people who would perform this music — white, suburbanite Catholic folk groups which would have to pretend that they were but poor, southern sharecroppers. The composer and the editors, sensing that the performers really had no instinctive 'feel' for this music, had to specify that the word 'Glory' was to be sung 'Glo (ho-ho)-ry, (hee)'. When I first beheld this printed text, I wanted to throw up, intellectually speaking.[2]

I used to belong to white suburbanite Christian music groups that were trying to imitate the music of poor southern sharecroppers![3] Back then I would have been angry at Mr Day's comments and called him a Pharisee for being so judgemental about sincere people who were only trying their best to serve God. But now I can see that he was devastatingly accurate; I have observed the same thing. I think it is a pathetic sight to behold a group of white Christians trying to 'get jiggy with it' (that is, attempting to perform music styles for which they are not culturally equipped) during the worship service. Exactly what glory does this bring to God? If Contemporaries really want to reach their oft-stated goal of 'authenticity' in worship, they would do well to perform only music at which they are 'authentically' good.

In all my experiences, I have met very few people who can interpret heavily syncopated melodies directly from sheet music without first hearing the song. I am one of those people. I also have a tendency towards making all music into a syncopated rock music song. This is an area of danger for me and one of the reasons why I am no longer leading or writing music in the church. When I led the worship, I had to teach others the melody by singing or playing it over and over again. Why do you think Contemporaries use projectors with the words only in place of sheet music? One unspoken reason is because the vast majority of congregations cannot read the heavily syncopated contemporary music.

Intimidated into silence

The second reason offered by discontented participants shocked me because I believed that our contemporary music ministry was, by definition, in touch with the average person in the pew. But some admitted they were intimidated into silence by the great singers in the worship team 'belting it out' on the platform. After all, what average congregation can compete with a group of gifted, microphoned vocalists blasting a melody from a stage, especially with an accompanying rock band? On the other hand, I found that hymn singing tends to level the playing field for the entire congregation by removing solo performances and concentrating instead on harmony.

Even 'seekers' and the 'unchurched' appreciate good hymn singing, and the spirit of harmony expressed by singing believers can be a powerful attraction to the gospel. Most of the unchurched I have met recognize the classic hymn tunes from childhood or from our culture (e.g. 'Amazing Grace', 'The Old Rugged Cross', 'How Great Thou Art', 'Holy, Holy, Holy', 'Just As I Am', to name but a few). They have told me how much they appreciate hearing these classic tunes, so much more than having to endure a watered-down, pale form of the music they listen to every day. Some have even expressed shock or confusion at hearing their 'worldly' music in church. This leads one to the conclusion that perhaps the Contemporaries are doing it simply for their own pleasure.

Is four-part hymn singing more beneficial to a congregation than singing melody-only CCM songs? I agree with the statement found in the Preface to *Christian Hymns*, the hymnbook used by evangelical churches in the United Kingdom:

Generally speaking, a congregation that is able to sing its hymns in four-part harmony will find — other things being equal — that its worship is richer and more satisfying than if it is able to sing only the melody of the hymns.[4]

Harmonizing hymn melodies in congregational singing is a beautiful thing to hear and to do. Why do we become swayed by the opinion that it is better to simplify the singing in our church? We seem to be only too willing to give up excellence and accept mediocrity. Most churches (even the seeker-sensitive) have people who can read music and who can help those who cannot; or the latter may simply stick to the familiar melody. This is what the church did for centuries before CCM proponents convinced us it was too difficult. Let's not give up so easily.

We can recapture the beauty and love of hymn singing in our churches if we follow the wise instructions found in John Wesley's *Rules for Methodist Singers* (abridged version).

1. Learn the tunes.
2. Sing them as printed.
3. Sing all. If it is a cross to you, take it up and you will find a blessing.
4. Sing lustily and with a good courage.
5. Sing modestly. Do not shout.
6. Sing in time. Do not run before or stay behind.
7. Above all, sing spiritually. Have an eye to God in every word you sing. Aim at pleasing him more than yourself or any other creature. In order to do this, attend strictly to the sense of what you sing, and see that your *heart* is not carried away with the sound, but offered to God continually.[5]

16.
Isn't God using CCM to save and disciple teens?

In chapter 12, we discussed the possible misuse of 1 Corinthians 9:22 ('I have become all things to all men, that I might by all means save some') to justify the use of any music style for evangelism. If you believe that this verse endorses the use of any music style as a means to reach the lost, then you will believe the argument in this chapter title, too.

There are a couple of problems with this argument. The first is tied to the application of 1 Corinthians 9:22. Can the use of an immoral and rebellious style of music be justified because it may help in the saving of sinners? Is that what draws sinners to Christ?

Of course not, but still the Contemporary asks: 'Why can't we use worldly music as a means to bring people in to hear the Word?' This question in and of itself typifies our basic problem. We sound like every rebellious group of believers throughout history. I hear echoes of backslidden Israel, whining and complaining to their leaders. Why can't we use some of the pagan rituals to worship *our* God? Why can't we sacrifice to *our* God on the high places, like they do? If we don't, our teenagers will get bored, reject our faith and become Philistines!

My friends, God does not want you to associate him with methods used by pagans for their immoral practices. He is a jealous God who demands in the first commandment that we stay away from idols (Exodus 20:3). He is also a loving God who knows what harm will come to us when we play around with immorality.

The second problem has been evident in our practical experience working with young people. What is the fruit produced in the lives of teenagers who use CCM? Judy and I once led a youth group at a Baptist church. We thought that CCM would be a good evangelism tool to reach the lost, and then help to disciple the saved teens. After all, the upbeat music appealed to them. We believed that CCM would help them understand spiritual concepts and keep them interested in church. We also wanted to provide an alternative to the world's music. We sincerely wanted to honour the Lord and minister to the young people.

We took teens to concerts given by popular CCM artists. These were not the 'radical' heavy metal or hip-hop artists, but the middle-of-the-road performers who seemed to be good role models. But we noticed that the artists, probably under the influence of their recording companies, imitated secular artists in music, concert performance techniques, dress, hairstyle and merchandising. Everything seemed to be geared to making money by winning fans. The poor teens were manipulated in the same way as when they were listening to their secular teen idols. They were hooked in the beginning by safe, careful lyrics and moderate music but the artists *always* progressed to an edgier, rockier and harder music style with a lifestyle and image to match. And the teens followed along.

The CCM artists became role models for different kinds of immorality: indecent dress, rebellious images, improper crushes on married men by young girls, lustful interest in sexy females by adolescent males. It makes no difference that the artists may not have intended this to happen or that they claimed their ministry for God rises above such things; a Christian performer in the public eye has a responsibility to, as Paul put it, 'give no offence in anything' (2 Corinthians 6:3). Instead, these artists allowed themselves to become 'idols' to the teens, often in the literal sense of encouraging worship.

Am I being unfair in making this charge of idol worship? Am I being too harsh? Not when we consider that the Greek word for idolatry literally means 'to worship *images*'. We saw how the teens worshipped the images of their favourite CCM artists: the life-size posters on their bedroom walls, showing the artist in a pose inspired by secular performers; the T-shirts with photos of the band; the screams of pleasure when the artist walked out on stage; and blatantly imitating the image of the CCM artist in their own dress and appearance. This behaviour does not conform to God's commandment in Exodus 20:4-5.

Because of what our experience has demonstrated and the Bible's strong warnings about idol worship, we are now opposed to using CCM as a ministry tool for teens because it only feeds their natural desires and passions; it does not produce the fruit of the Spirit. Even with the 'good Christian alternatives' we gave them, instead they craved more worldly music and their love for the world seemed to increase rather than decrease. We saw that godly disciplines of regular Bible study and prayer could not co-exist in their lives alongside the sensuality of CCM. Our conclusion was that the harm done to teens by CCM far outweighs any salvation or discipleship benefits. There are other proven ways to evangelize and disciple teens. We do not need CCM.

17.
Down the slippery slope
of blended services

Many churches have struggled, or are currently struggling, to accommodate the music desires of both the Contemporaries and the Traditionals. I am very much aware that pastors and music ministers in evangelical and fundamental churches have come under tremendous pressure from Contemporaries to compromise and allow CCM into the services. Out of this compromise was born the 'blended' worship service. This service combines musical elements of the old and the new together into one worship service.

Theoretically this should please everyone. Traditionals are initially assured by Contemporaries that the two styles can co-exist peacefully. In reality, what happens over time is a steady slide down the slippery slope, away from all traditional music into the latest, 'edgiest' contemporary styles.

How does a church get onto the slippery slope? I managed this change at two churches and will share my experiences. But first we need to understand how differently the Contemporary and the Traditional view the purpose of the worship service, and then compare what they expect to get out of it, respectively. We start with the common ground. Both sides sincerely want to honour and glorify God and Jesus Christ, and both are concerned that everyone derives some benefit from it. Then, as the following table illustrates, the objectives dramatically diverge.

	The Traditional	The Contemporary
What is the primary purpose of the worship service?	To prepare hearts for the preaching	To usher people into the presence of God
What tends to be emphasized?	The preaching	The music
What is the primary motive in selecting music?	Does God like it?	Do the people like it?
What is the secondary motive for selecting music?	Do the people like it?	Does God like it?
What is the primary indicator of a successful service?	I was really convicted by the Word of God today! (truth-based)	I really worshipped God today! (experience-based)

Now we will look at the progression of a blended service. It usually started very carefully with the inclusion of one or two Maranatha Music-style choruses in a Sunday evening service, such as 'Seek Ye First', 'Unto Thee O Lord', 'Glorify Thy Name', or 'I Love You Lord'. These are great praise songs and appropriate when a rock band does not accompany them. Sometimes the organist or pianist played the accompaniment, even though the songs were written for a cappella or acoustic guitar.

Then we might see the introduction of accompaniment tapes by soloists, most of which would include a muted but very contemporary-style drum and bass track. I found it unbelievable that a pastor who was dead-set against rock music, and preached that he would never allow a drum set in his church, would then allow musicians to sneak the drums and rock music in through the back door of accompaniment tapes. There was another side effect of using such tapes. Many gifted accompanists lost their personal ministry opportunity and became discouraged — more butterflies tossed onto the beach.

The first two steps were not enough to satisfy us. They simply whetted our appetites, and gave us the boldness to push for more contemporary music.

Next we looked for musical authenticity in the contemporary choruses. Most were not written to be played by our organist or pianist. They were written for guitars. So we brought in one acoustic guitar for the choruses. There is nothing wrong with that. I still believe that an acoustic guitar can be used for the glory of God in a service, as long as it is not used to create a rock beat or other sensual rhythm. As I write this, I am listening to a lovely classical guitar piece on the radio, reminding me of the beauty of this instrument for use in worship.

After we grew used to that, it made good sense that two guitars sounded better than one, and we may as well add the bass guitar too, along with its amplifier. This would also allow us to involve young Christian guitarists in ministry or even attract an unsaved guitarist to come to church: the same concept as the 'softball' ministry. Here was the humble beginning of the praise band in churches. This was also the point where the Traditionals began to complain loudly about the 'worldliness' in the church service.

When the drum set finally appeared on the platform, I believe the church reached the steepest and most dangerous part of the slope. More than any other instrument, a drum set is the key instrument of contemporary music styles. Drums are used to drive the beat, rock's true differentiation from other music styles. From this point on, the drums disproportionately influenced the music ministry. Music choices became more and more 'rocky' to satisfy the drummer (and those in the congregation attracted by this style). Services became louder and edgier. I have seen some worship leaders try in vain to control the drums by encasing the drum set in a Plexiglas sound barrier. But all that does is to bring more attention to the drums and make them look like a special object of worship.

At this point, let's stop and remember that we were trying to conduct a blended service to please the Traditionals too, so we still wanted some hymns using the organ and piano, and we still wanted to have a choir number. But by now we have decided to 'balance' the service by giving equal time to contemporary musicians.

Unwittingly, we have created an unnatural clash of incompatible musical styles unlike anything you would hear anywhere else in the world. With blended services, we have created two sets of musicians with different skills. Now began the competition for the hearts of the congregation: the battle of the bands, so to speak. Given the fact that we were already performing enough CCM to stir up the sinful nature of many in the congregation, it was predictable which style would win the battle. Contemporary always prevailed over Traditional, because it fed the sinful desire of our flesh. Add to that the veneer of respectability given to CCM by the leadership, and many believers gladly traded the old music for the new.

I tried in vain to be a bridge between the two styles, but there was, and there is, *no* middle ground. If I tried to tone down a contemporary song, the Contemporaries criticized me. If I arranged a hymn in a contemporary style, the Traditionals criticized me. As a musician, I discovered that any attempt to synthesize the two styles led to musical mediocrity and compromise. It was equally as inappropriate to play a contemporary chorus on the organ, as it was to play hymns with the band.

So I concluded that the two musical styles must remain separate, but could they be equal in the same service? No. As I showed in the table at the beginning of this chapter, the objectives and motives of each 'side' are incompatible; they cannot be *blended*. Eventually one will win out over the other. In our experience, the contemporary music gradually took over the service, and the traditional music became an occasional visitor, if it appeared at all. In contemporary services I've attended since, when the leader introduces a hymn in the middle of the set I can feel the disappointment or even a palpable sense of disdain emanating from Contemporaries in the congregation. 'Oh, do we really have to do *that* old song? Give us the new stuff so we can worship!' I fear that the classic hymns may disappear completely from our services within fifty years because younger generations have been raised on a steady diet of CCM. They are also told it is acceptable to use any new style and are given a continuous supply of subtle reasons why they do not need hymns.

I now believe that the blended service is not a long-term solution, despite being presented as such to the congregation by promoters of CCM. Rather, it is quite simply a transitional phase to gradually move a church service from all traditional to all contemporary. This process reminds me of the instructions on how to boil a live frog for dinner. If you drop the frog into a pot of boiling water, he will jump right back out every single time. But place him instead in a pot of lukewarm water and he'll feel comfortable and will stay there, happily floating along. If you then gradually increase the heat until the water boils, the poor frog won't notice the change until it is too late for him.

Some have tried to solve this dilemma by holding separate traditional and contemporary services. That addresses the problem of mixing incompatible music styles. But it can also become a breeding ground for division in the local church and it accommodates the use of inappropriate music styles without confronting the problem. Several churches in our area are experimenting with separate services; I am very curious to see the fruits produced over a period of time. But even this separation of services will not remain sharp for long. Soon it will blur, and the blurring is almost *always* towards contemporary shades.

Let me finish this chapter by telling you a sad story. At one of my churches, we had almost completed the slide into a totally contemporary style in every service and we had not used a hymnal in months. One weekend I was preparing for a Sunday that included observance of the Lord's Supper. There is very little contemporary music appropriate for this occasion, and even I, at this time in my musical journey, understood the need to be extra careful with music for a communion service. I was familiar with 1 Corinthians 11, where the apostle Paul warned us not to take the Lord's Supper lightly.

So I was led back into the hymnal that I kept nearby on our piano. The Lord prompted me to select 'Near the Cross'. At first I was going to put the words on the projector, but as I practised the song I heard the loveliest harmonies in my mind. I decided we would sing it out of the hymnal, giving people a chance to harmonize.

On Sunday morning, when it was time to prepare for communion, I asked the congregation to find a hymnal and turn to the correct page number. There was a brief moment of confusion; I heard murmuring and shuffling. Then I said to the congregation, 'You know, the blue book stuck under the pew in front of you.' But the auditorium lights were always dimmed during our worship time so that we could read the screen, and as a result some people could not find either the hymnal or the relevant page. I asked the crew to turn up the light.

What happened next was both sweet and sad. The light replaced the darkness and we sang out of the hymnals, with beautiful harmonies that brought tears of joy to my eyes and, from what I could see, to many other eyes in the congregation. The only accompaniment was a quiet piano. There were no drums or guitars or synthesizers to smother the singing of the saints.

Many times I have led hundreds in praise and worship, using both traditional and contemporary styles. But never before had I experienced such a sweet participation by *everyone* in the congregation. Every age group, no matter what their taste or preference, had been joined in a common song of repentance and praise to Jesus. Barriers came crashing down in this brief moment.

Then we put away the hymnals and dimmed the lights again.

18.
How then shall we worship together?

I have described some very serious problems introduced into our churches by the CCM movement. It is my prayer that every leader who has embraced the movement will seriously consider the need for a musical reformation.

We should *remove worldly CCM styles and influences from our services.* Consider all the benefits of this bold move.

1. There will be fewer divisions and church splits.
2. There will be less temptation for immorality.
3. There will be fewer tensions between members.
4. There will be less insensitivity towards each other.
5. There will be less compromise of our principles.
6. God will be pleased with all the above.

We should *return to traditional and non-controversial new music styles in our services.* Our church music should reflect beauty and peace. Philippians 4:8 has a list we should follow: 'Finally, brethren, whatever things are true, whatever things are noble, whatever things are just, whatever things are pure, whatever things are lovely, whatever things are of good report, if there is any virtue and if there is anything praiseworthy — meditate on these things.' How did we ever believe we could attain to whatever things are 'pure' by using CCM styles so closely associated with immorality and self-indulgence? Truth, virtue, purity and good reputation — these are ingredients missing from rock-influenced CCM with its worldly associations. Since holiness in every area of our conduct is what God demands (1 Peter 1:15), let's move closer to holiness in our choices for church music.

Instead of being 'edgy' and 'radical' with our praise and worship music, we should be very careful. We must understand that saints are literally those being sanctified or 'set apart' from the world for Christ's own glory. Therefore let us move *further* from worldliness in our music choices.

This is not an easy transition. CCM gains a stronghold in your heart and fights fiercely to keep you attached to it. The spirit of CCM affects everyone who is involved with it. Attempting to escape produces withdrawal pains. But God is faithful and just and forgives us, if we repent and confess our sins to him (1 John 1:9).

I have good news for the Contemporaries who are courageous enough to consider such a reformation. God inhabits the praise of his people without the presence of the latest CCM styles. I know this is true, because the church we currently attend has this kind of worship service.

The church's mission is to bring glory to God in all they do (1 Corinthians 10:31). There is a desire to please God with everything done in the services. Contrast this to the seeker-sensitive church, where every detail of the service is judged by how well it pleases *people*. Every aspect of ministry is expected to reflect the church's mission, including the music used in the services and throughout church life. The senior pastor has taken a very strong stand against the use of any CCM styles in the church. The associate pastor of music honours this stand with his music ministry.

At a typical service, you would see and hear:

- The great hymns of the faith sung out of hymnals and led by a songleader
- Enthusiastic congregational participation
- New praise and worship songs (but *none* that mimic CCM styles)
- A grand piano and an organ
- An orchestra with strings, brass and woodwinds
- An enthusiastic, well-rehearsed choir
- Soloists who sing with live accompanists
- Ensembles that emphasize harmony in song
- Culturally modest and respectful clothing worn by all musicians

Here is what you would *not* see or hear:

- CCM styles such as soft rock, easy listening rock, hard rock, smooth jazz, rap, or country & western
- A praise band with electric guitars and a drum set
- Musicians who mimic secular artists
- Lyrics projected up on a screen, in the place of real music
- An auditorium with dimmed lights
- Soloists who dress and sing like secular musicians
- Accompaniment tapes

The true spirit of worship

As a former worship leader, all of these musical details are important to me; but far more important to God is the *spirit of worship* at the church. As I mentioned earlier, when we worship we must learn how to humble our *hearts* before the great God. We must be in obedience to his Word before we can expect him to accept our sacrifice of praise. We must also be

diligent about personal holiness and avoid even a hint of immorality. While they are far from perfect, the church members
at least are serious about seeking these objectives. I have often
observed that when they are confronted with the glory and
awesomeness of God during a prayer, a song or a sermon, the
typical reaction is more of 'go to your knees' than 'lift up your
hands'.

What about the complaint from Contemporaries that the
traditional services are stuffy, ritualistic, dead or irrelevant? Is
there any truth at all to that complaint? If there is, what can the
Traditionals do to improve?

I must honestly confess there is some truth to this complaint.
As you have read by now, I began my musical experience as an
unsaved rock and roller; became a fundamentalist Traditional,
then a Contemporary advocate, and now I've returned to conservative church music. This variety of experience has given
me a unique perspective of all sides of the issue. In addition, I
have heard many other Traditionals admit they sometimes have
dead services.

Every Christian longs for, and deserves, the opportunity to
praise and worship God with an assembly of believers in a spirit
of unity. If Traditionals are clinging to old rituals or 'that's the
way we've always done it' attitudes that would hinder that, we
have an obligation to change for the better. We will never compromise God's principles and precepts! But we should want to
improve our efforts to glorify him in music. On the other hand,
we must avoid change for change's sake and not adopt any
new method that attempts to whip the people up into a 'wor-
shipful' or celebratory state. Whether it be the Contemporary's
New Age methods of dim lighting and rock music, or the Traditional's overbearing songleader who acts more like a cheer-
leader — I am equally opposed to such manipulation. Both
methods can and do produce 'fake' worshippers.

A warning to all

Finally, I have a warning for Contemporaries who are convicted to make a change and for Traditionals willing to take a stand in the church against CCM. When you decide to oppose CCM in the church, expect to be unfairly labelled by other Contemporaries as:

- a Pharisee
- a legalist
- placing traditions above Christ
- being insensitive to the needs of unbelievers
- having a judgemental spirit: 'Who are you to judge?'
- a hypocrite
- living in the past
- turning back the clock
- opposed to anything new

Contemporaries will use these convenient (and hurtful) labels in an attempt to marginalize and neutralize you. After all, what would happen to them if other people in your church paid attention to you and began to question the CCM status quo? They might lose their leadership and the power to determine the music used in the church. Even worse, you will expose their music philosophy as essentially man-centred.

Of course, be careful not to say and do things that would validate any of these labels. For example, base your objections on biblical grounds, not on man's reasoning. Don't quote Scripture out of context. Be gentle when you confront anyone. Ask Contemporaries to explain their motives and philosophies, rather than appear defensive. Stress that you are not opposed to all new music, only to music styles associated with immorality. Never use phrases like 'That's the way we've always done it.'

You will not be opposed by everyone. Expect some Contemporaries to sympathize with you in private. Many have experienced doubt about the music but go along with the leaders anyway. I have experienced this when discussing my book with former worship team partners. 'Yes,' they say to me in private, 'I agree that so and so is pushing the music envelope too far.' 'Yes, I am uncomfortable with the emphasis on performance.' Will they speak out in public? Maybe. But expect to walk this road alone for a while. It is a road less travelled, while the CCM highway is jam-packed.

Stay or leave?

What if you are in a church that has contemporary services and you see little hope of change? Should you stay in that church, or should you leave and find a church with a traditional service? This is easier said than done. In many areas of the world, most of the Bible-believing, Bible-preaching churches have gone over to contemporary or blended services, leaving you with few choices. At our church, we hear from members who have left the area due to career changes or college that it is very difficult to find another Bible-believing church with the same conviction of avoiding controversial CCM styles.

You may find it necessary to stay in your church and endure. Notice what Albert Barnes said on the subject of attending an imperfect church, in his New Testament commentary on Luke 4:16. Here, Barnes explains that the Lord Jesus regularly attended the synagogue services despite the corrupted doctrine and practices, and he draws two important conclusions about our duty to worship in public (italics mine).

And, as his custom was, he [Jesus] went. From this it appears that the Saviour regularly attended the service of the synagogue. In that service the Scriptures of the Old Testament were read, prayers were offered, and the Word of God was explained. There was great corruption in doctrine and practice at that time, but Christ did not on that account keep away from the place of public worship.

From this we may learn—

1st. That it is our duty regularly to attend public worship.

2nd. *That it is better to attend a place of worship which is not entirely pure, or where just such doctrines are not delivered as we would wish, than not attend at all.* It is of vast importance that the public worship of God should be maintained; and it is our duty to assist in maintaining it, to show by our example that we love it, and to win others also to love it. See Hebrews 10:25.

At the same time, this remark should not be construed as enjoining it as our duty to attend where the true God is not worshipped, or where he is worshipped with pagan rites and pagan prayers.[1]

To stay or to go is a personal or family decision that must be considered with much prayer. Whatever you decide, be careful not to fall into the trap of cynicism and scepticism about public worship and neglect your need to assemble regularly with other saints.

19.
How do we choose acceptable music for services?

This chapter is written mainly for the music minister who is struggling between Traditional and Contemporary music. I have long struggled with this question too. When I finally awoke to the problems of using contemporary music styles in church, I cried out to Judy, 'Well, then, tell me *what* music I should be using!' Earlier when I confronted Chris' youth pastor about the rock concert in church, he challenged me to come up with guidelines for what constitutes acceptable music. We are all looking for guidance.

I collect 'Worship Guidelines' from church websites to see what they are doing. At CCM churches, they typically go out of their way to praise their music diversity but I find no guidelines for what constitutes an appropriate music style. This should be no surprise to us by now, since we have seen that the very core of CCM philosophy denies that there can be *any* guidelines about music styles, because one is considered as good as another.

How can we objectively tell the difference between 'bad' and 'good' music? What are the guidelines we should use to choose appropriate and acceptable music for praise and worship? I personally wanted a manual on it. Our only standard for objectivity is the Bible. Humanly speaking, how I wish that God had left us a chapter defining acceptable church music! Some think he left us a Bible full of such music instruction but I cannot find enough detail that applies specifically to today's controversy. Our God, who spent so much time laying out the exact detail of the Tabernacle, could surely leave us a chapter (preferably in the New Testament) with verses that explicitly state: 'Do not use any music that the pagans are using today'; or 'These are the approved instruments — use no others'; or 'Thou shalt worship me only with music set to 6/8 time and no backbeat.' But he chose *not* to.

This fact begs the question: Have we elevated the place of church music in our worship to a level close to *idolatry*, to a level never intended by God? I believe both sides are guilty of this. Perhaps that is why God and Jesus were not more specific on how to conduct a New Testament church musical service. Maybe they wanted us to pay more attention to good preaching, a subject on which the Bible goes into great detail and one which we know God will use.

Let's face the facts then — as long as fallible man selects the music, there will be less than 100% objectivity. We should accept that some subjectivity will always be involved in music selection. If we do, then we can understand more readily why it is so important to learn the biblical principles for discerning questionable practices and avoiding evil that were covered in an earlier chapter on personal preferences. I also recommend a diligent study of 1 Chronicles 15 and 16 where David organized the musical structure of temple worship. This will help us to understand how a fallible man can become acceptable to God as a music minister before him, trusted to choose the music and the instruments wisely. A good introduction to this study is found in chapter 1 of Tim Fisher's *Music Discipleship*.

That said, here is my advice. First and foremost, anyone who chooses music for God's people should be concerned about his or her relationship with Jesus Christ. How is yours? Do you have a personal relationship with Jesus? Are you living a changed life as a result? Do you live with any unconfessed sin that hinders your spiritual discernment?

Next, because we serve a holy God who demands separation from the world for his ministers (1 Peter 1:15), we must be very careful with our own personal music preferences. We cannot listen to secular or Christian rock and roll all day long and then expect to choose service music that is acceptable to God. The same goes for other forms of secular and Christian music, including (sorry, friends) country & western. When we bathe our ears in these styles, we become tainted by the world and it will affect our music choices. In my case, you read how a steady diet of Promise Keeper music and CCM classic rock styles inevitably became the dominant music I chose for the service.

Now assuming that those important issues have been dealt with, here are some of my practical 'in the trenches' suggestions for anyone who wants to reform their services.

1. *Learn to live by the principles.* All music used in church should be selected using the biblical principles discussed earlier in this book. It should not have any hint of immorality (guilt by association) and it should not be offensive to other Christians. Wait a minute, Dan — are you saying that if only *one* person is offended, even if I don't really like that person and I know he is the weaker brother, I need to submit to his wishes? No, I am saying that *we need to get the beam out of our own eye first* so we can see clearly what our brother needs.

2. *If it's got that swing, it ain't good to sing!* I mean Christian soft rock, P&W tunes, hard rock, country rock, easy jazz, pop rock, rap, hip-hop, reggae, ska, blues, big band and all other forms influenced by rock. I hope by now you have

seen clear and understandable reasons for this. If you are wondering if a particular song has a rock beat influence and cannot determine it by yourself, send me an e-mail and I'll help. I can spot that backbeat a mile away.

3. *Break up the praise band.* Without drums and electric guitars to influence you, it will be very hard to choose the wrong music. De-emphasize the beat and you will often find that there is not much left in a CCM piece. Put the traditional musicians back in there and see what happens. As an additional benefit, you will also greatly please the elder members and the classically trained musicians of your church. What do you say to the praise band members? Give them a copy of this book.

4. *If you think the music might offend someone, it probably will, so ASK FIRST!* Contemporaries have an aggravating habit of 'Sing first, ask questions later.' And then they wonder why some people develop resentment. Don't restrict your research only to the members of the worship team and everyone else who thinks exactly like you. Ask the opinion of at least one person who is ten years older than you.

5. *Hymns are usually safe and sound.* There are some great and powerful hymns that will lead people to worship God just as effectively as any new Integrity Hosanna praise song. Yes, I know the Contemporary comeback here, that some hymns are not theologically pure; but if you are a Christian leader, you should be able to discern that. Don't throw out the baby with the bath water.

6. *Contemporary songs are acceptable, as long as the emphasis is not on a syncopated beat, but on melody and harmony.* That in effect rules out the vast majority of today's CCM or

P&W music, which are heavily dominated by a syncopated beat. But fear not, because there are many good songs out there that you have missed because you spent so much time being a Contemporary and living in their world. E-mail me for some suggestions. And of course, the lyrics must be doctrinally sound just like the hymns you choose.

7. *Use music for congregational singing, not just words on a screen.* Stop treating your congregation as a group of music illiterates. Every church has a sufficient number of members who can read music. If you don't have music for everyone, then buy it! Remember those old hymnals? They have four-part songs so everyone can harmonize and find a comfortable part. When you make this change, you will also solve another irritating problem. At services that use only words on the screen, I often hear people trying to harmonize but they are making it up because they don't remember the right notes or they never learned the music. This leads to bad singing and clashing notes. That is not music done decently and in order. Give those who want to harmonize the notes to read!

8. *Put the microphones back on the stands.* Take the mikes out of the hands of the singers. Handheld mikes encourage a performance style that emphasizes the performer, which often leads musicians to mimic secular entertainers in style and fashion and to desire music that is performance-oriented.

Conclusion

C. S. Lewis once commented that when a person is walking in the wrong direction, sometimes the best way to make progress is to turn around, go back and get on the right road.[1] He was trying to point out that moving ahead is not always progress in the qualitative sense of the word. For the past two or three decades Christian music has taken giant steps — but, I believe, in the wrong direction. It's time to turn around — or, as the Bible puts it, to repent.

I have shown from my experience that CCM's acceptance into the church came into being out of our self-indulgence and lusts, that it has been justified by deceptive arguments, and that it is fuelled by our desire for music that feeds our sinful nature. We have been deceived into believing that we can use any style of music in our worship service and that God accepts it. This is false! Our acceptance of this lie has harmed an entire generation of older Christians, has split churches, and is encouraging immorality, self-indulgence and divisive attitudes in the church.

But the bottom line to all of this boils down to one thing. We have an active enemy called Satan and he wants to erode the effectiveness of the local church from the inside out. So far, I think he has made excellent progress with music controversies. But I trust in the Lord Jesus Christ to expose this and help us to overcome it. I claim the promise of 1 John 4:4: 'You are of God, little children, and have overcome them, because he who is in you is greater than he who is in the world.'

I have written this book because Judy and I want to rescue the butterflies that were wounded and hurt in the storm of the Contemporary Praise & Worship movement. Butterflies, let us know if we have encouraged you. I also hope that leaders and followers of this movement have had their eyes opened by God to see the spiritual and emotional damage caused by the CCM storm. I welcome a respectful and honest dialogue with anyone who has comments or questions. Please contact me at danlucarini@msn.com.

May our great and gracious God grant us *all* repentance from worldliness and give us the will to reform our worship practices, so that they are pleasing and acceptable to him!

Notes

Chapter 2
1. City-wide, non-denominational prayer meetings held throughout the United States in the 1990s.
2. Rick Warren, *The Purpose Driven Church*, p.285.

Chapter 3
1. John Makujina, *Measuring the Music*, p.208.
2. Warren, *The Purpose Driven Church*, p.279.
3. *Ibid*. p.280.
4. *Matthew Henry Commentary on the Whole Bible*.
5. This is a twist on the oft-seen sticker displayed on the car bumpers of gun owners in America, and is analogous to the more familiar phrase 'over my dead body'.

Chapter 4
1. Zodhiates, *The Complete Word Study Dictionary, New Testament*, 1992, p.1233.
2. Albert Barnes, *New Testament Commentary*.
3. Bob Hudson © 1978 Maranatha! Music.
4. Steven John Camp, *A call for reformation in the Contemporary Christian Music industry*.
5. © 1999 Kingsway Thank You Music.

Chapter 5
1. John MacArthur, *Ashamed of the Gospel*, p.46.
2. Al Mohler Jr, excerpt from his paper delivered at the Alliance of

Confessing Evangelicals' meeting in Cambridge, MA, April 1996. © 1996, 1999 Alliance of Confessing Evangelicals.
3. A. W. Tozer, *The pursuit of God*, Preface. © 1948 (expired) by Christian Publications.
4. Cambridge Declaration of the Alliance of Confessing Evangelicals, *Thesis Five*.
5. MacArthur, *Ashamed of the Gospel*, p.46.

Chapter 6
1. From 'The Erotic vs. the Spiritual' in *Born After Midnight*, pp.37-8. It was originally published in 1959, reprinted in 1989 by Christian Publications in Camp Hill, PA.

Chapter 7
1. Warren, *The Purpose Driven Church*, p.280.
2. A proportion of the profits from this book go to missions projects sponsored by Evangelical Press.

Chapter 9
1. *Contemporary Christian Music*, November 1988, p.12.
2. Warren, *Purpose Driven Church*, p.281.

Chapter 13
1. Definitions taken from *Strong's Concordance*.
2. Matthew Henry's *Commentary on the Whole Bible*.

Chapter 14
1. Makujina, *Measuring the Music*, pp.192-3.
2. *Ibid.* pp.201-2.

Chapter 15
1. Spring of Life Community Church, Hawaii. *Guidelines for Worship Gatherings*, as e-mailed to me from the pastor.
2. *Why Catholics Can't Sing*, p.59.
3. Tenant farmers in the American Deep South who give a part of their crop as rent: known for their rhythm and blues style music, one of rock and roll's influences.

4. *Christian Hymns* © 1977 Evangelical Movement of Wales.
5. Preface to *Christian Hymns*, p.5.

Chapter 18
1. Albert Barnes, *New Testament Commentary*.

Conclusion
1. C. S. Lewis, *Mere Christianity*, p.36.

CAN WE

ROCK

THE GOSPEL?

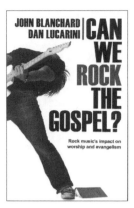

Few subjects generate more heat in the Christian church today than the use of music in worship and evangelism. Every musical form and every way of expressing it has as many detractors as it does promoters. Yet in recent years most of the conflicts have centred on what is generically known as rock music, which has become an increasingly dominant — and divisive — issue since it first slipped into church life some forty years ago.

For some Christians it is by far the best way of expressing their faith and of sharing it with unbelievers, while for other Christians it is by far the worst. Does the truth lie somewhere between these two extremes? Does God endorse music of every kind? Can we 'cut and paste' secular rock music and 'Christianize' it in the process? Should the Christian church unite in bringing rock music to the altar or in sending it to the bonfire?

Two respected Christian leaders and best-selling authors who together have many years of hands-on experience in worship, preaching, evangelism and music have combined to produce a book that examines this controversial subject, using both recent evidence and time-tested truths.

They come to a clear conclusion. They will not leave you neutral.

John Blanchard and Dan Lucarini, Evangelical Press, 272 pages, ISBN-13 978-0-85234-628-0.

A wide range of excellent books on spiritual subjects is available from Evangelical Press. Please write to us for your free catalogue or contact us by e-mail. Alternatively, you can view the whole catalogue online at our web site:

www.evangelicalpress.org

Evangelical Press
Faverdale North, Darlington, DL3 0PH, England

e-mail: sales@evangelicalpress.org

Evangelical Press USA
P. O. Box 825, Webster, New York 14580, USA

e-mail: usa.sales@evangelicalpress.org